THE NATION'S FAVOURITE POEMS OF DESIRE

Also available from BBC Worldwide:

The Nation's Favourite Poems
ISBN: 0 563 38782 3
ISBN: 0 563 38487 5 (hardback gift edition)

The Nation's Favourite Love Poems
ISBN: 0 563 38378 X
ISBN: 0 563 38432 8 (hardback gift edition)

The Nation's Favourite Comic Poems
ISBN: 0 563 38451 4

The Nation's Favourite Twentieth Century Poems
ISBN: 0 563 55143 7

The Nation's Favourite Shakespeare
ISBN: 0 563 55142 9

The Nation's Favourite Poems of Childhood
ISBN: 0 563 55184 4

The Nation's Favourite Children's Poems
ISBN: 0 563 53774 4

The Nation's Favourite Poems of Animals
ISBN: 0 563 53780 9

The Nation's Favourite Poems of Journeys
ISBN: 0 563 53715 9

Audio cassettes available from BBC Radio Collection

The Nation's Favourite Poems
ISBN: 0 563 38987 7

The Nation's Favourite Love Poems
ISBN: 0 563 38279 1

The Nation's Favourite Comic Poems
ISBN: 0 563 55850 4

The Nation's Favourite Shakespeare
ISBN: 0 563 55331 6

The Nation's Favourite Lakeland Poems
ISBN: 0 563 55293 X

The Nation's Favourite Poems of Childhood
ISBN: 0 563 47727 X

The above titles are also available on CD

THE NATION'S FAVOURITE POEMS OF DESIRE

—◇—

FOREWORD BY

MARIELLA FROSTRUP

Published by
BBC Worldwide Limited,
Woodlands,
80 Wood Lane,
London
W12 0TT

First published 2003
Edited by Alex Warwick

ISBN: 0 563 48834 4

Set in Stempel Garamond by Keystroke,
Jacaranda Lodge, Wolverhampton.
Printed and bound in Great Britain by Martins the Printers Ltd,
Berwick-upon-Tweed.
Cover printed by Belmont Press, Northampton.

THE POETRY SOCIETY

CONTENTS

— ◇ —

'I know not what to do'

'And Thou beside me singing'

'five minutes left before the world begins'

'Yet come to me in dreams'

'There is no bliss like this'

'Th' expense of spirit in a waste of shame'

'is there Beauty yet to find?'

FOREWORD

BY MARIELLA FROSTRUP

— ◇ —

We (women) know a thing or two about desire. Biblically, our sex is defined by our lack of resistance to it. From the moment Eve reached out for that luscious, all too tempting apple we were marked out as the weaker sex, incapable of resisting temptation, who for our own good had to have our uncontrollable appetites kept in check. That was a very long time ago. These days we've shaken off that repressive chador and are free to express our desire in its myriad forms. There are some who would argue that the fairer sex explain it best, but I think both sexes have their moments of inspiration. In the *Lord of the Rings* trilogy, Tolkien powerfully depicts how night falls on the world when our darkest desires take hold of our hearts. Bob Dylan and U2 have paid musical homage to the power of desire. On screen, Buñuel spoke to all the lustlorn in *That Obscure Object of Desire* when his hero, Fernando Rey, carried the weight of his desire in a sack on his back. Who hasn't felt that same heavy load of longing at some time in their lives?

Desire is the emotion that sets us apart from the rest of the animal kingdom. We are ruled by it, yet, ironically, it's that irrational appetite for anything from an ice cream to an empire to a fellow human being, that has led us to becoming the masters of our small part of the universe. We humans are driven mad by desire, made sick with it, commit our worst crimes in its name and yet, when our desire is sated, we experience happiness like no other creature. Consumed with desire we are at our most human and least predictable. It's a constant battle between the darkness and the light, which only ends in some form of consummation.

Desire is not only elusive, uncontrollable and unpredictable. For the common-or-garden *Homo sapiens*, it's also almost impossible to put into words. We make do with 'I love...' and 'I want...' when what we're trying to express is the most complicated of all urges. Poetry is desire's chosen language and remains the perfect form for expressing our secret longings. From Catullus to Cavafy, the Greeks were masters of the art, but we moderns also have an enviable canon of poems dedicated to the subject. This collection highlights some of the greatest poems of desire in the English language. It's a wonderful collection that allows us to embark on a voyage on the turbulent seas of the human heart without even getting our feet wet.

'Infinite passion, and the pain
Of finite hearts that yearn'

ALFRED, LORD TENNYSON 1809–92

from IN MEMORIAM

Thy voice is on the rolling air;
I hear thee where the waters run;
Thou standest in the rising sun,
And in the setting thou art fair.

What are thou then? I cannot guess;
But though I seem in star and flower
To feel thee some diffusive power,
I do not therefore love thee less:

My love involves the love before;
My love is vaster passion now;
Though mixed with God and Nature thou,
I seem to love thee more and more.

Far off thou art, but ever nigh;
I have thee still, and I rejoice;
I prosper, circled with thy voice;
I shall not lose thee though I die.

MATTHEW ARNOLD 1822–88

TO MARGUERITE

Yes! in the sea of life enisled,
    With echoing straits between us thrown,
Dotting the shoreless watery wild,
    We mortal millions live *alone*.
The islands feel the enclasping flow,
And then their endless bounds they know.

But when the moon their hollows lights,
    And they are swept by balms of spring,
And in their glens, on starry nights,
    The nightingales divinely sing;
And lovely notes, from shore to shore,
Across the sounds and channels pour –

Oh! then a longing like despair
Is to their farthest caverns sent;
For surely once, they feel, we were
    Parts of a single continent!
Now round us spreads the watery plain –
Oh might our marges meet again!

Who ordered, that their longing's fire
Should be, as soon as kindled, cooled?
Who renders vain their deep desire? –
A God, a God their severance ruled!
And bade betwixt their shores to be
The unplumbed, salt, estranging sea.

EMILY DICKINSON 1830–86

249

Wild Nights – Wild Nights!
Were I with thee
Wild Nights should be
Our luxury!

Futile – the Winds –
To a Heart in port –
Done with the Compass –
Done with the Chart!

Rowing in Eden –
Ah, the Sea!
Might I but moor – Tonight –
In Thee!

CHARLOTTE MEW 1869–1928

ON THE ROAD TO THE SEA

We passed each other, turned and stopped for half an hour, then went our way,
I who make other women smile did not make you –
But no man can move mountains in a day.
So this hard thing is yet to do.

But first I want your life: – before I die I want to see
The world that lies behind the strangeness of your eyes,
There is nothing gay or green there for my gathering, it may be,
Yet on brown fields there lies
A haunting purple bloom: is there not something in grey skies
And in grey sea?
I want what world there is behind your eyes,
I want your life and you will not give it me.

Now, if I look, I see you walking down the years,
Young, and through August fields – a face, a thought, a swinging dream perched on a stile – ;
I would have liked (so vile we are!) to have taught you tears
But most to have made you smile.

Today is not enough or yesterday: God sees it all –
Your length on sunny lawns, the wakeful rainy nights – ; tell
me – ; (how vain to ask), but it is not a question – just a call – ;
Show me then, only your notched inches climbing up the garden wall,
I like you best when you are small.

Is this a stupid thing to say
Not having spent with you one day?
No matter; I shall never touch your hair
Or hear the little tick behind your breast,
Still it is there,
And as a flying bird
Brushes the branches where it may not rest
I have brushed your hand and heard
The child in you: I like that best

So small, so dark, so sweet; and were you also then too grave and wise?
Always I think. Then put your far off little hand in mine; – Oh! let it rest;
I will not stare into the early world beyond the opening eyes,
Or vex or scare what I love best.
But I want your life before mine bleeds away –
Here – not in heavenly hereafters – soon, –
I want your smile this very afternoon,
(The last of all my vices, pleasant people used to say,
I wanted and I sometimes got – the Moon!)

You know, at dusk, the last bird's cry,
And round the house the flap of the bat's low flight,
Trees that go black against the sky
And then – how soon the night!

Now shadow of you on any bright road again,
And at the darkening end of this – what voice? Whose kiss? As if you'd say!
It is not I who have walked with you, it will not be I who take away
Peace, peace, my little handful of the gleaner's grain
From your reaped fields at the shut of day.

Peace! Would you not rather die
Reeling, – with all the cannons at your ear?
So, at least, would I.
And I may not be here
Tonight, tomorrow morning or next year.
Still I will let you keep your life a little while,
See dear?
I have made you smile.

JOHN KEATS 1795–1821

LA BELLE DAME SANS MERCI

Oh, what can ail thee, knight-at-arms,
   Alone and palely loitering?
The sedge has withered from the lake,
   And no birds sing!

Oh, what can ail thee, knight-at-arms,
   So haggard and so woe-begone?
The squirrel's granary is full,
   And the harvest's done.

I see a lily on thy brow,
   With anguish moist and fever-dew,
And on thy cheek a fading rose
   Fast withereth too.

I met a lady in the meads
   Full beautiful, a fairy's child,
Her hair was long, her foot was light,
   And her eyes were wild.

I made a garland for her head,
   And bracelets too, and fragrant zone;
She looked at me as she did love,
   And made sweet moan.

I set her on my pacing steed,
   And nothing else saw all day long;
For sidelong would she bend, and sing
   A fairy's song.

She found me roots of relish sweet,
   And honey wild, and manna dew;
And sure in language strange she said,
   'I love thee true'.

She took me to her elfin grot,
   And there she wept, and sighed full sore,
And there I shut her wild wild eyes
   With kisses four.

And there she lullèd me asleep,
   And there I dreamed – Ah! woe betide! –
The latest dream I ever dreamed
   On the cold hill side.

I saw pale kings, and princes too,
   Pale warriors, death-pale were they all;
They cried – 'La belle Dame sans merci
   Hath thee in thrall!'

I saw their starved lips in the gloam
   With horrid warning gapèd wide,
And I awoke, and found me here
   On the cold hill side.

And this is why I sojourn here,
   Alone and palely loitering,
Though the sedge is withered from the lake,
   And no birds sing.

ALFRED, LORD TENNYSON 1809–92

MARIANA

With blackest moss the flower-plots
  Were thickly crusted, one and all:
The rusted nails fell from the knots
  That held the pear to the garden-wall.
The broken sheds look'd sad and strange:
  Unlifted was the clinking latch;
  Weeded and worn the ancient thatch
Upon the lonely moated grange.
    She only said, 'My life is dreary,
      He cometh not,' she said;
    She said, 'I am aweary, aweary,
      I would that I were dead!'

Her tears fell with the dews at even;
  Her tears fell ere the dews were dried;
She could not look on the sweet heaven,
  Either at morn or eventide.
After the flitting of the bats,
  When thickest dark did trance the sky,
  She drew her casement-curtain by,
And glanced athwart the glooming flats.
    She only said, 'The night is dreary,
      He cometh not,' she said;
    She said, 'I am aweary, aweary,
      I would that I were dead!'

Upon the middle of the night,
  Waking she heard the night-fowl crow:
The cock sung out an hour ere light:
  From the dark fen the oxen's low
Came to her: without hope of change,
  In sleep she seem'd to walk forlorn,
  Till cold winds woke the grey-eyed morn
About the lonely moated grange.

She only said, 'The day is dreary,
He cometh not,' she said;
She said, 'I am aweary, aweary,
I would that I were dead!'

About a stone-cast from the wall
A sluice with blacken'd waters slept,
And o'er it many, round and small,
The cluster'd marish-mosses crept.
Hard by a poplar shook alway,
All silver-green with gnarled bark:
For leagues no other tree did mark
The level waste, the rounding grey.
She only said, 'My life is dreary,
He cometh not,' she said;
She said, 'I am aweary, aweary,
I would that I were dead!'

And ever when the moon was low,
And the shrill winds were up and away,
In the white curtain, to and fro,
She saw the gusty shadows sway.
But when the moon was very low,
And wild winds bound within their cell,
The shadow of the poplar fell
Upon her bed, across her brow.
She only said, 'The night is dreary,
He cometh not,' she said;
She said, 'I am aweary, aweary,
I would that I were dead!'

All day within the dreamy house,
The doors upon their hinges creak'd;
The blue fly sung in the pane; the mouse
Behind the mouldering wainscot shriek'd,
Or from the crevice peer'd about.
Old faces glimmer'd thro' the doors,
Old footsteps trod the upper floors,
Old voices called her from without.
She only said, 'My life is dreary,
He cometh not,' she said;
She said, 'I am aweary, aweary,
I would that I were dead!'

The sparrow's chirrup on the roof,
The slow clock ticking, and the sound
Which to the wooing wind aloof
The poplar made, did all confound
Her sense; but most she loathed the hour
When the thick-moted sunbeam lay
Athwart the chambers, and the day
Was sloping toward his western bower.
Then, said she, 'I am very dreary,
He will not come,' she said;
She wept, 'I am aweary, aweary,
O God, that I were dead!'

NAOMI LONG MADGETT 1932–

BLACK WOMAN

My hair is springy like the forest grasses
That cushion the feet of squirrels–
Crinkled and blown in a south breeze
Like the small leaves of native bushes.

My black eyes are coals burning
Like a low, full, jungle moon
Through the darkness of being.
In a clear pool I see my face,
Know my knowing.

My hands move pianissimo
Over the music of the night:
Gentle birds fluttering through leaves and grasses
They have not always loved,
Nesting, finding home.

Where are my lovers?
Where are my tall, my lovely princes
Dancing in slow grace
Toward knowledge of my beauty?
Where
Are my beautiful
Black men?

ROBERT BROWNING 1812–89

TWO IN THE CAMPAGNA

1

I wonder do you feel today
As I have felt since, hand in hand,
We sat down on the grass, to stray
In spirit better through the land,
This morn of Rome and May?

2

For me, I touched a thought, I know,
Has tantalized me many times,
(Like turns of thread the spiders throw
Mocking across our path) for thymes
To catch at and let go.

3

Help me to hold it! First it left
The yellowing fennel, run to seed
There, branching from the brickwork's cleft,
Some old tomb's ruin: yonder weed
Took up the floating weft,

4

Where one small orange cup amassed
Five beetles—blind and green they grope
Among the honey-meal: and last,
Everywhere on the grassy slope
I traced it. Hold it fast!

5

The champaign with its endless fleece
Of feathery grasses everywhere!
Silence and passion, joy and peace,
An everlasting wash of air—
Rome's ghost since her decease.

6

Such life here, through such lengths of hours,
   Such miracles performed in play,
Such primal naked forms of flowers,
   Such letting nature have her way
While heaven looks from its towers!

7

How say you? Let us, O my dove,
   Let us be unashamed of soul,
As earth lies bare to heaven above!
   How is it under our control
To love or not to love?

8

I would that you were all to me,
   You that are just so much, no more.
Nor yours nor mine, nor slave nor free!
   Where does the fault lie? What the core
O' the wound, since wound must be?

9

I would I could adopt your will,
   See with your eyes, and set my heart
Beating by yours, and drink my fill
   At your soul's springs—your part my part
In life, for good and ill.

10

No. I yearn upward, touch you close,
   Then stand away. I kiss your cheek,
Catch your soul's warmth—I pluck the rose
   And love it more than tongue can speak—
Then the good minute goes.

11

Already how am I so far
    Out of that minute? Must I go
Still like the thistle-ball, no bar,
    Onward, whenever light winds blow,
Fixed by no friendly star?

12

Just when I seemed about to learn!
    Where is the thread now? Off again!
The old trick! Only I discern—
    Infinite passion, and the pain
Of finite hearts that yearn.

CHARLOTTE MEW 1869–1928

THE FARMER'S BRIDE

Three Summers since I chose a maid,
Too young maybe – but more's to do
At harvest-time than bide and woo.
  When us was wed she turned afraid
Of love and me and all things human;
Like the shut of a winter's day.
Her smile went out, and 'twasn't a woman –
  More like a little frightened fay.
    One night, in the Fall, she runned away.

'Out 'mong the sheep, her be,' they said,
'Should properly have been abed;
But sure enough she wasn't there
Lying awake with her wide brown stare.
So over seven-acre field and up-along across the down
We chased her, flying like a hare
Before our lanterns. To Church-Town
  All in a shiver and a scare
We caught her, fetched her home at last
  And turned the key upon her, fast.

She does the work about the house
As well as most, but like a mouse:
  Happy enough to chat and play
  With birds and rabbits and such as they,
  So long as men-folk keep away.

'Not near, not near!' her eyes beseech
When one of us comes within reach.
  The women say that beasts in stall
  Look round like children at her call.
  I've hardly heard her speak at all.

Shy as a leveret, swift as he,
Straight and slight as a young larch tree,
Sweet as the first wild violets, she,
To her wild self. But what to me?

The short days shorten and the oaks are brown,
  The blue smoke rises to the low grey sky,
One leaf in the still air falls slowly down,
  A magpie's spotted feathers lie
On the black earth spread white with rime,
The berries redden up to Christmas-time.
  What's Christmas-time without there be
  Some other in the house than we!

  She sleeps up in the attic there
  Alone, poor maid. 'Tis but a stair
Betwixt us. Oh! my God! the down,
The soft young down of her, the brown,
The brown of her – her eyes, her hair, her hair!

KATHLEEN JAMIE 1962–

JULIAN OF NORWICH

Everything I do I do for you.
Brute. You inform the dark
inside of stones, the winds draughting in

from this world and that to come,
but never touch me.
You took me on

but dart like a rabbit into holes
from the edges of my sense
when I turn, walk, turn.

*

I am the hermit whom you keep
at the garden's end, but I wander.
I am wandering in your acres

where every step, were I
attuned to sense them,
would crush a thousand flowers.

(Hush, that's not the attitude)
I keep prepared a room and no one comes.
(Love is the attitude)

*

Canary that I am, caged and hung
from the eaves of the world
to trill your praise.

He will not come.
Poor bloodless hands, unclasp.
Stiffened, stone-cold knees, bear me up.

(And yet, and yet, I am suspended
in his joy, huge and helpless
as the harvest moon in a summer sky.)

CAROL ANN DUFFY 1955–

WARMING HER PEARLS

Next to my own skin, her pearls. My mistress
bids me wear them, warm them, until evening
when I'll brush her hair. At six, I place them
round her cool, white throat. All day I think of her,

resting in the Yellow room, contemplating silk
or taffeta, which gown tonight? She fans herself
whilst I work willingly, my slow heat entering
each pearl. Slack on my neck, her rope.

She's beautiful. I dream about her
in my attic bed; picture her dancing
with tall men, puzzled by my faint persistent scent
beneath her French perfume, her milky stones.

I dust her shoulders with a rabbit's foot,
watch the soft blush seep through her skin
like an indolent sigh. In her looking-glass
my red lips part as though I want to speak.

Full moon. Her carriage brings her home. I see
her every movement in my head . . . Undressing,
taking off her jewels, her slim hand reaching
for the case, slipping naked into bed, the way

she always does . . . And I lie here awake,
knowing the pearls are cooling even now
in the room where my mistress sleeps. All night
I feel their absence and I burn.

EDNA ST VINCENT MILLAY 1892–1950

FIRST FIG

My candle burns at both ends;
  It will not last the night;
But ah, my foes, and oh, my friends—
  It gives a lovely light!

SIR JOHN BETJEMAN 1906–84

MYFANWY

Kind o'er the *kinderbank* leans my Myfanwy,
   White o'er the play-pen the sheen of her dress,
Fresh from the bathroom and soft in the nursery
   Soap-scented fingers I long to caress.

Were you a prefect and head of your dormit'ry?
   Were you a hockey girl, tennis or gym?
Who was your favourite? Who had a crush on you?
   Which were the baths where they taught you to swim?

Smooth down the Avenue glitters the bicycle,
   Black-stockinged legs under navy-blue serge,
Home and Colonial, Star, International,
   Balancing bicycle leant on the verge.

Trace me your wheel-tracks, you fortunate bicycle,
   Out of the shopping and into the dark,
Back down the Avenue, back to the pottingshed,
   Back to the house on the fringe of the park.

Golden the light on the locks of Myfanwy,
   Golden the light on the book on her knee,
Finger-marked pages of Rackham's Hans Andersen,
   Time for the children to come down to tea.

Oh! Fuller's angel-cake, Robertson's marmalade,
   Liberty lampshade, come, shine on us all,
My! what a spread for the friends of Myfanwy
   Some in the alcove and some in the hall.

Then what sardines in the half-lighted passages!
   Locking of fingers in long hide-and-seek.
You will protect me, my silken Myfanwy,
   Ringleader, tom-boy, and chum to the weak.

WILLIAM WORDSWORTH 1770–1850

SURPRISED BY JOY

Surprised by joy—impatient as the Wind
I turned to share the transport—Oh! with whom
But thee, deep buried in the silent tomb,
That spot which no vicissitude can find?
Love, faithful love, recalled thee to my mind—
But how could I forget thee? Through what power,
Even for the least division of an hour,
Have I been so beguiled as to be blind
To my most grievous loss!—That thought's return
Was the worst pang that sorrow ever bore,
Save one, one only, when I stood forlorn,
Knowing my heart's best treasure was no more;
That neither present time, nor years unborn
Could to my sight that heavenly face restore.

ROBERT BROWNING 1812–89

IN THREE DAYS

So, I shall see her in three days
And just one night, but nights are short,
Then two long hours, and that is morn.
See how I come, unchanged, unworn!
Feel, where my life broke off from thine,
How fresh the splinters keep and fine, –
Only a touch and we combine!

Too long, this time of year, the days!
But nights, at least the nights are short.
As night shows where her one moon is,
A hand's-breadth of pure light and bliss,
So life's night gives my lady birth
And my eyes hold her! What is worth
The rest of heaven, the rest of earth?

O loaded curls, release your store
Of warmth and scent, as once before
The tingling hair did, lights and darks
Outbreaking into fairy sparks,
When under curl and curl I pried
After the warmth and scent inside,
Thro' lights and darks how manifold –
The dark inspired, the light controlled!
As early Art embrowns the gold.

What great fear, should one say, 'Three days
That change the world might change as well
Your fortune; and if joy delays,
Be happy that no worse befell!'
What small fear, if another says,
'Three days and one short night beside
May throw no shadow on your ways;
But years must teem with change untried,

With chance not easily defied,
With an end somewhere undescried.'
No fear! – or if a fear be born
This minute, it dies out in scorn.
Fear? I shall see her in three days
And one night, now the nights are short,
Then just two hours, and that is morn.

RICHARD LOVELACE 1618–57/8

TO ALTHEA, FROM PRISON

When Love with unconfinèd wings
Hovers within my gates;
And my divine Althea brings
To whisper at the grates;
When I lie tangled in her hair,
And fettered to her eye;
The Gods that wanton in the air
Know no such liberty.

When flowing cups run swiftly round
With no allaying Thames,
Our careless heads with roses bound
Our hearts with loyal flames;
When thirsty grief in wine we steep,
When healths and draughts go free,
Fishes that tipple in the deep
Know no such liberty.

When, like committed linnets, I
With shriller throat shall sing
The sweetness, mercy, majesty,
And glories of my King;
When I shall voice aloud how good
He is, how great should be,
Enlargèd wings that curl the flood
Know no such liberty.

Stone walls do not a prison make,
  Nor iron bars a cage;
Minds innocent and quiet take
  That for an hermitage;
If I have freedom in my love,
  And in my soul am free;
Angels alone that soar above
  Enjoy such liberty.

'If I meet
you suddenly, I can't
speak'

JOHN CLARE 1793–1864

FIRST LOVE

I ne'er was struck before that hour
With love so sudden and so sweet
Her face it bloomed like a sweet flower
And stole my heart away complete
My face turned pale a deadly pale
My legs refused to walk away
And when she looked what could I ail
My life and all seemed turned to clay

And then my blood rushed to my face
And took my eyesight quite away
The trees and bushes round the place
Seemed midnight at noon day
I could not see a single thing
Words from my eyes did start
They spoke as chords do from the string
And blood burnt round my heart

Are flowers the winters choice
Is love's bed always snow
She seemed to hear my silent voice
Not loves appeal to know
I never saw so sweet a face
As that I stood before
My heart has left its dwelling place
And can return no more –

EMILY DICKINSON 1830–86

315

He fumbles at your Soul
As Players at the Keys
Before they drop full Music on –
He stuns you by degrees –
Prepares your brittle Nature
For the Etherial Blow
By fainter Hammers – further heard –
Then nearer – Then so slow
Your Breath has time to straighten –
Your Brain – to bubble cool –
Deals – One – imperial – Thunderbolt –
That scalps your naked Soul –

When Winds take Forests in their Paws –
The Universe – is still –

LORD GEORGE GORDON BYRON 1788–1824

from DON JUAN, CANTO II

A long, long kiss, a kiss of youth, and love,
  And beauty, all concentrating like rays
Into one focus, kindled from above;
  Such kisses as belong to early days,
Where heart, and soul, and sense, in concert move,
  And the blood's lava, and the pulse a blaze,
Each kiss a heart-quake – for a kiss's strength,
I think, it must be reckoned by its length.

By length, I mean duration; theirs endured
  Heaven knows how long – no doubt they never reckoned;
And if they had, they could not have secured
  The sum of their sensations to a second:
They had not spoken; but they felt allured,
  As if their souls and lips each other beckoned,
Which, being joined, like swarming bees they clung –
Their hearts the flowers from whence the honey sprung.

They were alone, but not alone as they
  Who shut in chambers think it loneliness;
The silent ocean, and the starlit bay,
  The twilight glow, which momently grew less,
The voiceless sands, and dropping caves, that lay
  Around them, made them to each other press,
As if there were no life beneath the sky
Save theirs, and that their life could never die.

They feared no eyes nor ears on that lone beach,
  They felt no terrors from the night; they were
All in all to each other; though their speech
  Was broken words, they *thought* a language there –
And all the burning tongues the passions teach
  Found in one sigh the best interpreter
Of nature's oracle – first love – that all
Which Eve has left her daughters since her fall.

PATRICK MACDONOGH 1902–60

SHE WALKED UNAWARE

Oh, she walked unaware of her own increasing beauty
That was holding men's thoughts from market or plough,
As she passed by intent on her womanly duties
And she passed without leisure to be wayward or proud;
Or if she had pride then it was not in her thinking
But thoughtless in her body like a flower of good breeding.
The first time I saw her spreading coloured linen
Beyond the green willow she gave me gentle greeting
With no more intention than the leaning willow tree.

Though she smiled without intention yet from that day forward
Her beauty filled like water the four corners of my being,
And she rested in my heart like a hare in the form
That is shaped to herself. And I that would be singing
Or whistling at all times went silently then,
Till I drew her aside among straight stems of beeches
When the blackbird was sleeping and she promised that never
The fields would be ripe but I'd gather all sweetness,
A red moon of August would rise on our wedding.

October is spreading bright flame along stripped willows,
Low fires of the dogwood burn down to grey water, –
God pity me now and all desolate sinners
Demented with beauty! I have blackened my thought
In drouths of bad longing, and all brightness goes shrouded
Since he came with his rapture of wild words that mirrored
Her beauty and made her ungentle and proud.
Tonight she will spread her brown hair on his pillow,
But I shall be hearing the harsh cries of wild fowl.

ELLEN BRYANT VOIGT 1943–

WHY SHE SAYS NO

Two friends at the close of summer.
On the path, the birds quicken.
While he talks,
he strokes her arm in one direction
as if it had a nap of feathers.
How handsomely the heart's valves
lie open for the bloodrush.
How her body also begins to open.
At the edge of the woods, they pass
goldenrod and lupin, the tall thin weeds
supple as a whale's teeth
conducting the avid fish to the interior.

She is not the mouth, whatever you think
and even though she craves
this closeness, its rich transfusion.
Desire is the mouth, the manipulating heart,
the wing. Above her,
the branches of the pines, their quilled expanse
blanketing the subtler vegetation.

MARY BARNARD 1932–63

FRAGMENT THIRTY-NINE

He is more than a hero. – Sappho

He is a god in my eyes –
the man who is allowed
to sit beside you – he

who listens intimately
to the sweet murmur of
your voice, the enticing

laughter that makes my own
heart beat fast. If I meet
you suddenly, I can't

speak – my tongue is broken;
a thin flame runs under
my skin; seeing nothing,

hearing only my own ears
drumming, I drip with sweat;
trembling shakes my body

and I turn paler than
dry grass. At such times
death isn't far from me

GEOFFREY CHAUCER 1340?–1400

from MERCILESS BEAUTY

Your eyen two will slay me suddenly;
I may the beauty of them not sustain,
So woundeth it throughout my hearte keen.

And but your word will healen hastily
My hearte's wounde, while that it is green,
    Your eyen two will slay me suddenly;
    I may the beauty of them not sustain.

Upon my truth I say you faithfully
That ye bin of my life and death the queen;
For with my death the truthe shall be seen.
    Your eyen two will slay me suddenly;
    I may the beauty of them not sustain,
    So woundeth it throughout my hearte keen.

JOHN KEATS 1795–1821

'I CRY YOUR MERCY'

I cry your mercy– pity– love! aye, love!
Merciful love that tantalizes not,
One-thoughted, never-wandering, guileless love,
Unmasked, and being seen– without a blot!
O! let me have thee whole,– all– all– be mine!
That shape, that fairness, that sweet minor zest
Of love, your kiss,– those hands, those eyes divine,
That warm, white, lucent, million-pleasured breast,–
Yourself– your soul– in pity give me all,
Withhold no atom's atom or I die,
Or living on perhaps, your wretched thrall,
Forget, in the midst of idle misery,
Life's purposes,– the palate of my mind
Losing its gust, and my ambition blind!

THOMAS LYNCH 1948–

MAURA

She had never desired him in that way –
that aching in the skin she'd sometimes get
for a man possessed of that animal something.

Something outside of language or regret. No,
he'd been the regular husband, the hedged bet
against the baglady and spinsterhood;

a cap on the toothpaste, the mowed lawn, bills paid;
a well-insured warm body in the bed,
the kindly touch if seldom kindling.

Odd then, to have a grief so passionate
it woke her damp from dreams astraddle him –
the phantom embraced in pillow and blankets,

or sniffed among old shirts and bureau drawers.
She fairly swooned sometimes remembering
the curl of her name in his dull tenor.

Sweet nothings now rewhispered in her ears.
She chose black lace, black satin, reckoning
such pain a kind of romance in reverse.

The house filled with flowers. She ate nothing.
Giddy and sleepless, she longed for him alone.
Alone at last, she felt a girl again.

'I know not what to do'

JOHN DONNE 1572–1631

THE BAITE

Come live with mee, and bee my love,
And we will some new pleasures prove
Of golden sands, and christall brookes,
With silken lines, and silver hookes.

There will the river whispering runne
Warm'd by thy eyes, more then the Sunne.
And there th' inamor'd fish will stay,
Begging themselves they may betray.

When thou wilt swimme in that live bath,
Each fish, which every channell hath,
Will amorously to thee swimme,
Gladder to catch thee, then thou him.

If thou, to be so seene, beest loath,
By Sunne, or Moone, thou darknest both,
And if my selfe have leave to see,
I need not their light, having thee.

Let others freeze with angling reeds,
And cut their legges, with shells and weeds,
Or treacherously poore fish beset,
With strangling snare, or windowie net:

Let coarse bold hands, from slimy nest
The bedded fish in banks out-wrest,
Or curious traitors, sleavesilke flies
Bewitch poore fishes wandring eyes.

For thee, thou needst no such deceit,
For thou thy selfe art thine owne bait;
That fish, that is not catch'd thereby,
Alas, is wiser farre then I.

ANDREW MARVELL 1621–78

TO HIS COY MISTRESS

Had we but world enough, and time,
This coyness, lady, were no crime.
We would sit down, and think which way
To walk, and pass our long love's day.
Thou by the Indian Ganges' side
Shoudst rubies find; I by the tide
Of Humber would complain. I would
Love you ten years before the flood,
And you should, if you please, refuse
Till the conversion of the Jews.
My vegetable love should grow
Vaster than empires and more slow;
An hundred years should go to praise
Thine eyes, and on thy forehead gaze;
Two hundred to adore each breast,
But thirty thousand to the rest;
An age at least to every part,
And the last age should show your heart.
For, lady, you deserve this state,
Nor would I love at lower rate.
But at my back I always hear
Time's wingèd chariot hurrying near;
And yonder all before us lie
Deserts of vast eternity.
Thy beauty shall no more be found;
Nor, in thy marble vault, shall sound
My echoing song, then worms shall try
That long-preserved virginity,
And your quaint honor turn to dust,
And into ashes all my lust:
The grave's a fine and private place,
But none, I think, do there embrace.
Now therefore, while the youthful hue
Sits on thy skin like morning dew,

And while thy willing soul transpires
At every pore with instant fires,
Now let us sport us while we may,
And now, like amorous birds of prey,
Rather at once our time devour
Than languish in his slow-chapped power.
Let us roll all our strength and all
Our sweetness up into one ball,
And tear our pleasures with rough strife
Through the iron gates of life:
Thus, though we cannot make our sun
Stand still, yet we will make him run.

JOHN DONNE 1572–1631

TO HIS MISTRESS GOING TO BED

Come, Madam, come, all rest my powers defy,
Until I labour, I in labour lie.
The foe oft-times, having the foe in sight,
Is tired with standing, though they never fight.
Off with that girdle, like heaven's zone glistering
But a far fairer world encompassing.
Unpin that spangled breast-plate, which you wear
That th'eyes of busy fools may be stopped there:
Unlace yourself, for that harmonious chime
Tells me from you that now 'tis your bed time.
Off with that happy busk, whom I envy
That still can be, and still can stand so nigh.
Your gown's going off such beauteous state reveals
As when from flowery meads th'hills shadow steals.
Off with your wiry coronet and show
The hairy diadem which on you doth grow.
Off with those shoes: and then safely tread
In this love's hallowed temple, this soft bed.
In such white robes heaven's angels used to be
Received by men; thou Angel bring'st with thee
A heaven like Mahomet's Paradise; and though
Ill spirits walk in white, we easily know
By this these Angels from an evil sprite:
They set out hairs, but these the flesh upright.
   Licence my roving hands, and let them go
Behind, before, above, between, below.
Oh my America, my new found land,
My kingdom, safeliest when with one man manned,
My mine of precious stones, my Empery,
How blessed am I in this discovering thee.
To enter in these bonds is to be free,
Then where my hand is set my seal shall be.
   Full nakedness, all joys are due to thee.
As souls unbodied, bodies unclothed must be

To taste whole joys. Gems which you women use
Are as Atlanta's balls, cast in men's views,
That when a fool's eye lighteth on a gem
His earthly soul may covet theirs not them.
Like pictures, or like books' gay coverings made
For laymen, are all women thus arrayed;
Themselves are mystic books, which only we
Whom their imputed grace will dignify
Must see revealed. Then since I may know,
As liberally as to a midwife show
Thyself; cast all, yea this white linen hence.
Here is no penance, much less innocence.
　To teach thee, I am naked first: Why then
What need'st thou have more covering than a man.

THOMAS MOORE 1779–1852

DID NOT

'Twas a new feeling – something more
Than we had dared to own before,
   Which then we hid not;
We saw it in each other's eye,
And wished, in every half-breathed sigh,
   To speak, but did not.

She felt my lips' impassioned touch –
'Twas the first time I dared so much,
   And yet she chid not;
But whispered o'er my burning brow,
'Oh, do you doubt I love you now?'
   Sweet soul! I did not.

Warmly I felt her bosom thrill,
I pressed it closer, closer still,
   Though gently bid not;
Till – oh! the world hath seldom heard
Of lovers, who so nearly erred,
   And yet, who did not.

THOMAS HARDY 1840–1928

A THUNDERSTORM IN TOWN

(A Reminiscence: 1893)

She wore a new 'terra-cotta' dress,
And we stayed, because of the pelting storm,
Within the hansom's dry recess,
Though the horse had stopped; yea, motionless
        We sat on, snug and warm.

Then the downpour ceased, to my sharp sad pain
And the glass that had screened our forms before
Flew up, and out she sprang to her door:
I should have kissed her if the rain
        Had lasted a minute more.

H.D. (HILDA DOOLITTLE) 1886–1921

FRAGMENT THIRTY-SIX

I know not what to do: my mind is divided. – Sappho

I know not what to do,
my mind is reft:
is song's gift best?
is love's gift loveliest?
I know not what to do,
now sleep has pressed
weight on your eyelids.

Shall I break your rest,
devouring, eager?
is love's gift best?
nay, song's the loveliest:
yet were you lost,
what rapture
could I take from song?
what song were left?

I know not what to do:
to turn and slake
the rage that burns,
with my breath burn
and trouble your cool breath?
so shall I turn and take
snow in my arms?
(is love's gift best?)
yet flake on flake
of snow were comfortless,
did you lie wondering,
wakened yet unawake.

Shall I turn and take
comfortless snow within my arms?
press lips to lips
that answer not,
press lips to flesh
that shudders not nor breaks?

Is love's gift best?
shall I turn and slake
all the wild longing?
O I am eager for you!
as the Pleiads shake
white light in whiter water
so shall I take you?

My mind is quite divided,
my minds hesitate,
so perfect matched,
I know not what to do:
each strives with each
as two white wrestlers
standing for a match,
ready to turn and clutch
yet never shake muscle nor nerve nor tendon;
so my mind waits
to grapple with my mind,
yet I lie quiet,
I would seem at rest.

I know not what to do:
strain upon strain,
sound surging upon sound
makes my brain blind;
as a wave-line may wait to fall
yet (waiting for its falling)
still the wind may take
from off its crest,
white flake on flake of foam,
that rises,
seeming to dart and pulse
and rend the light,
so my mind hesitates
above the passion
quivering yet to break,
so my mind hesitates
above my mind,
listening to song's delight.

I know not what to do:
will the sound break,
rending the night
with rift on rift of rose
and scattered light?
will the sound break at last
as the wave hesitant,
or will the whole night pass
and I lie listening awake?

T.S. ELIOT 1885–1965

LA FIGLIA CHE PIANGE

O quam te memorem virgo

Stand on the highest pavement of the stair –
Lean on a garden urn –
Weave, weave the sunlight in your hair –
Clasp your flowers to you with a pained surprise –
Fling them to the ground and turn
With a fugitive resentment in your eyes:
But weave, weave the sunlight in your hair.

So I would have had him leave,
So I would have had her stand and grieve,
So he would have left
As the soul leaves the body torn and bruised,
As the mind deserts the body it has used.
I should find
Some way incomparably light and deft,
Some way we both should understand,
Simple and faithless as a smile and shake of the hand.

She turned away, but with the autumn weather
Compelled my imagination many days,
Many days and many hours:
Her hair over her arms and her arms full of flowers.
And I wonder how they should have been together!
I should have lost a gesture and a pose.
Sometimes these cognitions still amaze
The troubled midnight and the noon's repose.

'And Thou beside me singing'

WILLIAM WORDSWORTH 1770–1850

SHE WAS A PHANTOM OF DELIGHT

She was a Phantom of delight
When first she gleamed upon my sight;
A lovely Apparition, sent
To be a moment's ornament;
Her eyes as stars of Twilight fair;
Like Twilight's, too, her dusky hair;
But all things else about her drawn
From May-time and the cheerful Dawn;
A dancing Shape, an Image gay,
To haunt, to startle, and way-lay.

I saw her upon nearer view,
A Spirit, yet a Woman too!
Her household motions light and free,
And steps of virgin-liberty;
A countenance in which did meet
Sweet records, promises as sweet;
A Creature not too bright or good
For human nature's daily food;
For transient sorrows, simple wiles,
Praise, blame, love, kisses, tears, and smiles.

And now I see with eye serene
The very pulse of the machine;
A Being breathing thoughtful breath,
A Traveler between life and death;
The reason firm, the temperate will,
Endurance, foresight, strength, and skill;
A perfect Woman, nobly planned,
To warn, to comfort, and command;
And yet a Spirit still, and bright
With something of angelic light.

ROBERT HERRICK 1591–1674

DELIGHT IN DISORDER

A sweet disorder in the dresse
Kindles in cloathes a wantonnesse:
A Lawne about the shoulders thrown
Into a fine distraction: –
An erring Lace, which here and there
Enthralls the Crimson Stomacher: –
A Cuffe neglectfull, and thereby
Ribbands to flow confusedly: –
A winning wave (deserving Note)
In the tempestuous petticote: –
A careless shoe-string, in whose tye
I see a wilde civility: –
Doe more bewitch me, than when Art
Is too precise in every part.

GEORGE MEREDITH 1828–1909

from LOVE IN THE VALLEY

This I may know: her dressing and undressing
  Such a change of light shows as when the skies in sport
Shift from cloud to moonlight; or edging over thunder
  Slips a ray of sun; or sweeping into port
White sails furl; or on the ocean borders
  White sails lean along the waves leaping green.
Visions of her shower before me, but from eyesight
  Guarded she would be like the sun were she seen.

* * * * * *

O the golden sheaf, the rustling treasure-armful!
  O the nutbrown tresses nodding interlaced!
O the treasure-tresses one another over
  Nodding! O the girdle slack about the waist!
Slain are the poppies that shot their random scarlet,
  Quick amid the wheatears: wound about the waist,
Gathered, see these brides of Earth one blush of ripeness!
  O the nutbrown tresses nodding interlaced!

PETER REDGROVE 1932–

SWEAT

I sit in the hot room and I sweat,
I see the cool pane bedew with me,
My skin breathes out and pearls the windowpane,
Likes it and clings to it. She comes in,
She loves me and she loves our children too,
And still the sweat is trickling down the pane,
The breath of life makes cooling streaks
And wobbles down the pane. We breathe and burn,
We burn, all together in a hot room,
Our sweat is smoking down the windowpane,
Marks time. I smoke, I stir, and there I write
PR, BR, a streaming heart.
The sun strikes at it down a wide hollow shaft;
Birds swing on the beams, boil off the grass.

JOHN BERRYMAN 1914–72

from THE DREAM SONGS

Filling her compact & delicious body
with chicken páprika, she glanced at me
twice.
Fainting with interest, I hungered back
and only the fact of her husband & four other people
kept me from springing on her

or falling at her little feet and crying
'You are the hottest one for years of night
Henry's dazed eyes
have enjoyed, Brilliance.' I advanced upon
(despairing) my spumoni. – Sir Bones: is stuffed,
de world, wif feeding girls.

– Black hair, complexion Latin, jeweled eyes
downcast . . . The slob beside her   feasts . . . What wonders is
she sitting on, over there?
The restaurant buzzes. She might as well be on Mars.
Where did it all go wrong? There ought to be a law against Henry.
– Mr. Bones: there is.

ROBERT HERRICK 1591–1674

UPON JULIA'S CLOTHES

Whenas in silks, my Julia goes,
Then, then, methinks, how sweetly flows
That liquefaction of her clothes!

Next, when I cast mine eyes, and see
That brave vibration, each way free,
– O, how that glittering taketh me!

ANON

from THE SONG OF SOLOMON

I am the rose of Sharon, and the lily of the valleys.

As the lily among thorns, so is my love among the daughters.

As the apple tree among the trees of the wood, so is my beloved among the sons. I sat down under his shadow with great delight, and his fruit was sweet to my taste.

He brought me to the banqueting house, and his banner over me was love.

Stay me with flagons, comfort me with apples: for I am sick of love.

His left hand is under my head, and his right hand doth embrace me.

I charge you, O ye daughters of Jerusalem, by the roes, and by the hinds of the field, that ye stir not up, nor awake my love, till he please.

The voice of my beloved! behold, he cometh leaping upon the mountains, skipping upon the hills.

My beloved is like a roe or a young hart: behold, he standeth behind our wall, he looketh forth at the windows, showing himself through the lattice.

My beloved spake, and said unto me, Rise up, my love, my fair one, and come away.

For, lo, the winter is past, the rain is over and gone;

The flowers appear on the earth; the time of the singing of birds is come, and the voice of the turtle is heard in our land:

The fig tree putteth forth her green figs, and the vines with the tender grape give a good smell. Arise, my love, my fair one, and come away.

O my dove, that art in the clefts of the rock, in the secret places of the stairs, let me see thy countenance, let me hear thy voice; for sweet is thy voice, and thy countenance is comely.

Take us the foxes, the little foxes, that spoil the vines; for our vines have tender grapes.

My beloved is mine, and I am his: he feedeth among the lilies.

Until the day break, and the shadows flee away, turn, my beloved, and be thou like a roe or a young hart upon the mountains of Bether.

EDWARD FITZGERALD 1809–83

from THE RUBAIYAT OF OMAR KHAYYAM

A Book of Verses underneath the Bough,
A Jug of Wine, a Loaf of Bread—and Thou
  Beside me singing in the Wilderness—
Oh, Wilderness were Paradise enow!

CONNIE BENSLEY 1929–

DESIRES

Newly shaven, your eyes only slightly bloodshot,
Your rat-trap mouth smiling up at the corners,
You remind me of the Head Girl
I used to be in love with.

It's something about your sporty build,
The way you seem to be counting the people in the café
With a view to lining them up in teams.

It's quite set me in the mood for the evening,
And I follow you alertly through the door,
Hoping you'll turn and snap at me
To pick my feet up, and not to slouch.

WENDY COPE 1945–

SONG

My love got in the car
And sat on my banana,
My unobserved banana
And my organic crisps.

We spoke of life and love,
His rump on my banana,
My hidden, soft banana
And my forgotten crisps.

He kissed me more than once
As he sat on that banana,
That newly-squashed banana
And those endangered crisps.

We looked up at the stars –
Beneath him, my banana,
My saved-from-lunch banana
And my delicious crisps.

At last I dropped him off
And noticed the banana –
Alas, a ruined banana
And sadly damaged crisps.

You'd think he would have felt
A fairly large banana
And, if not the banana,
The lumpy bag of crisps.

But he's the kind of man
Who'll sit on a banana
For hours. Watch your banana
And guard your bag of crisps.

He waved goodbye and smiled,
Benign as a banana.
'I love you, daft banana,'
Said I, and ate the crisps.

SEAMUS HEANEY 1939–

FIELD WORK

I

Where the sally tree went pale in every breeze,
where the perfect eye of the nesting blackbird watched,
where one fern was always green

I was standing watching you
take the pad from the gatehouse at the crossing
and reach to lift a white wash off the whins.

I could see the vaccination mark
stretched on your upper arm, and smell the coal smell
of the train that comes between us, a slow goods,

waggon after waggon full of big-eyed cattle.

II

But your vaccination mark is on your thigh,
an O that's healed into the bark.

Except a dryad's not a woman
you are my wounded dryad

in a mothering smell of wet
and ring-wormed chestnuts.

Our moon was small and far,
was a coin long gazed at

brilliant on the *Pequod*'s mast
across Atlantic and Pacific waters.

III

Not the mud slick,
not the black weedy water
full of alder cones and pock-marked leaves.

Not the cow parsley in winter
with its old whitened shins and wrists,
its sibilance, its shaking.

Not even the tart green shade of summer
thick with butterflies
and fungus plump as a leather saddle.

No. But in a still corner,
braced to its pebble-dashed wall,
heavy, earth-drawn, all mouth and eye,

the sunflower, dreaming umber.

IV

Catspiss smell,
the pink bloom open:
I press a leaf
of the flowering currant
on the back of your hand
for the tight slow burn
of its sticky juice
to prime your skin,
and your veins to be crossed
criss-cross with leaf-veins.
I lick my thumb
and dip it in mould,
I anoint the anointed
leaf-shape. Mould
blooms and pigments
the back of your hand
like a birthmark –
my umber one,
you are stained, stained
to perfection.

GRACE NICHOLS 1950–

THOSE WOMEN

Cut and contriving women
hauling fresh shrimps
up in their seines

standing waist deep
in the brown voluptuous
water of their own element

how I remember those women
sweeping in the childish rivers
of my eyes

and the fish slipping
like eels
through their laughing thighs

'five minutes left before the world begins'

HELEN DUNMORE 1952–

PRIVACY OF RAIN

Rain. A plump splash
on tense, bare skin.
Rain. All the May leaves
run upward, shaking.

Rain. A first touch
at the nape of the neck.
Sharp drops kick the dust, white
downpours shudder
like curtains, rinsing
tight hairdos to innocence.

I love the privacy of rain,
the way it makes things happen
on verandahs, under canopies
or in the shelter of trees
as a door slams and a girl runs out
into the black-wet leaves.
By the brick wall an iris
sucks up the rain
like intricate food, its tongue
sherbetty, furred.

Rain. All the May leaves
run upward, shaking.
On the street, bud-silt
covers the windscreens.

THEODORE ROETHKE 1908–63

THE VOICE

One feather is a bird,
I claim; one tree, a wood;
In her low voice I heard
More than a mortal should;
And so I stood apart,
Hidden in my own heart.

And yet I roamed out where
Those notes went, like the bird,
Whose thin song hung in air,
Diminished, yet still heard:
I lived with open sound,
Aloft, and on the ground.

That ghost was my own choice,
The shy cerulean bird;
It sang with her true voice,
And it was I who heard
A slight voice reply;
I heard; and only I.

Desire exults the ear:
Bird, girl, and ghostly tree,
The earth, the solid air –
Their slow song sang in me;
The long noon pulsed away,
Like any summer day.

HELEN DUNMORE 1952–

DANCING MAN

That lake lies along the shore
like a finger down my cheek,

its waters lull and collapse
dark as pomegranates,

the baby crawls on the straw
in the shadow-map of his father's chair

while the priest talks things over
and light dodges across his hair.

There's a lamp lit in the shed
and a fire on, and a man drinking

spiritus fortis he's made for himself.
But on the floor of the barn

the dancing man is beginning to dance.
First a beat from the arch of his foot

as he stands upright, a neat
understatement of all that's in him

and he lowers his eyes to her
as if it's nothing, nothing –

but she has always wanted him.
Her baby crawls out from the chairs

and rolls in his striped vest laughing
under the feet of the dancers

so she must dance over him
toe to his cheek, heel to his hair,

as she melts to the man dancing.
They are talking and talking over there –

the priest sits with his back to her
for there's no malice in him

and her husband glistens like the sun
through the cypress-flame of the man dancing.

In the shed a blackbird
has left three eggs which might be kumquats –

they are so warm. One of them's stirring –
who said she had deserted them?

In the orchard by the barn
there are three girls wading,

glossy, laughing at something,
they spin a bucket between them,

glowing, they are forgotten –
something else is about to happen.

ANNA WICKHAM 1884–1947

THE FIRED POT

In our town, people live in rows.
The only irregular thing in a street is the steeple;
And where that points to, God only knows,
And not the poor disciplined people!

And I have watched the women growing old,
Passionate about pins, and pence, and soap,
Till the heart within my wedded breast grew cold,
And I lost hope.

But a young soldier came to our town,
He spoke his mind most candidly.
He asked me quickly to lie down,
And that was very good for me.
For though I gave him no embrace –
Remembering my duty –
He altered the expression of my face,
And gave me back my beauty.

ROBERT BROWNING 1812–89

MEETING AT NIGHT

The grey sea and the long black land;
And the yellow half-moon large and low;
And the startled little waves that leap
In fiery ringlets from their sleep,
As I gain the cove with pushing prow,
And quench its speed i' the slushy sand.

Then a mile of warm sea-scented beach;
Three fields to cross till a farm appears;
A tap at the pane, the quick sharp scratch
And blue spurt of a lighted match,
And a voice less loud, thro' its joys and fears,
Than the two hearts beating each to each!

LOUIS MACNEICE 1907–63

MEETING POINT

Time was away and somewhere else,
There were two glasses and two chairs
And two people with the one pulse
(Somebody stopped the moving stairs):
Time was away and somewhere else.

And they were neither up nor down;
The stream's music did not stop
Flowing through heather, limpid brown,
Although they sat in a coffee shop
And they were neither up nor down.

The bell was silent in the air
Holding its inverted poise –
Between the clang and clang a flower,
A brazen calyx of no noise:
The bell was silent in the air.

The camels crossed the miles of sand
That stretched around the cups and plates;
The desert was their own, they planned
To portion out the stars and dates:
The camels crossed the miles of sand.

Time was away and somewhere else.
The waiter did not come, the clock
Forgot them and the radio waltz
Came out like water from a rock:
Time was away and somewhere else.

Her fingers flicked away the ash
That bloomed again in tropic trees:
Not caring if the markets crash
When they had forests such as these,
Her fingers flicked away the ash.

God or whatever means the Good
Be praised that time can stop like this,
That what the heart has understood
Can verify in the body's peace
God or whatever means the Good.

Time was away and she was here
And life no longer what it was,
The bell was silent in the air
And all the room one glow because
Time was away and she was here.

ROBERT GRAVES 1895–1985

GIFT OF SIGHT

I had long known the diverse tastes of the wood,
Each leaf, each bark, rank earth from every hollow;
Knew the smells of bird's breath and of bat's wing;
Yet sight I lacked: until you stole upon me,
Touching my eyelids with light finger-tips.
The trees blazed out, their colours whirled together,
Nor ever before had I been aware of sky.

ELIZABETH BISHOP 1911–79

THE SHAMPOO

The still explosions on the rocks,
the lichens, grow
by spreading, gray, concentric shocks.
They have arranged
to meet the rings around the moon, although
within our memories they have not changed.

And since the heavens will attend
as long on us,
you've been, dear friend,
precipitate and pragmatical;
and look what happens. For Time is
nothing if not amenable.

The shooting stars in your black hair
in bright formation
are flocking where,
so straight, so soon?
– Come, let me wash it in this big tin basin,
battered and shiny like the moon.

MAYA ANGELOU 1928–

AFTER

No sound falls
from the moaning sky
No scowl wrinkles
the evening pool
    The stars lean down
    A stony brilliance
    While birds fly.

The market leers
its empty shelves
Streets bare bosoms
to scanty cars
    This bed yawns
    beneath the weight
    of our absent selves.

LESLEÁ NEWMAN 1955–

POSSIBLY

to wake and find you sitting up in bed
with your black hair and gold skin
leaning against the white wall
a perfect slant of sunlight slashed
across your chest as if God
were Rembrandt or maybe Ingmar Bergman
but luckily it's too early to go to the movies
and all the museums are closed on Tuesday
anyway I'd rather be here with you
than in New York or possibly Amsterdam
with our eyes and lips and legs and bellies
and the sun as big as a house in the sky
and five minutes left before the world begins

TED HUGHES 1930–98

SEPTEMBER

We sit late, watching the dark slowly unfold:
No clock counts this.
When kisses are repeated and the arms hold
There is no telling where time is.

It is midsummer: the leaves hang big and still:
Behind the eye a star,
Under the silk of the wrist a sea, tell
Time is nowhere.

We stand; leaves have not timed the summer.
No clock now needs
Tell we have only what we remember:
Minutes uproaring with our heads

Like an unfortunate King's and his Queen's
When the senseless mob rules;
And quietly the trees casting their crowns
Into the pools.

'Yet come to me in dreams'

CHRISTINA ROSSETTI 1830–94

ECHO

Come to me in the silence of the night;
Come in the speaking silence of a dream;
Come with soft rounded cheeks and eyes as bright
As sunlight on a stream;
Come back in tears,
O memory, hope and love of finished years.

O dream how sweet, too sweet, too bitter-sweet,
Whose wakening should have been in Paradise,
Where souls brim-full of love abide and meet;
Where thirsting longing eyes
Watch the slow door
That opening, letting in, lets out no more.

Yet come to me in dreams, that I may live
My very life again though cold in death;
Come back to me in dreams, that I may give
Pulse for pulse, breath for breath:
Speak low, lean low,
As long ago, my love, how long ago.

JOHN KEATS 1795–1821

from THE EVE OF ST AGNES

Then by the bed-side, where the faded moon
Made a dim, silver twilight, soft he set
A table, and, half anguish'd, threw thereon
A cloth of woven crimson, gold, and jet: –
O for some drowsy Morphean amulet!
The boisterous, midnight, festive clarion,
The kettle-drum, and far-heard clarionet,
Affray his ears, though but in dying tone: –
The hall door shuts again, and all the noise is gone.

And still she slept an azure-lidded sleep,
In blanched linen, smooth, and lavender'd,
While he from forth the closet brought a heap
Of candied apple, quince, and plum, and gourd;
With jellies soother than the creamy curd,
And lucent syrops, tinct with cinnamon;
Manna and dates, in argosy transferr'd
From Fez; and spiced dainties, every one,
From silken Samarcand to cedar'd Lebanon.

These delicates he heap'd with glowing hand
On golden dishes and in baskets bright
Of wreathed silver: sumptuous they stand
In the retired quiet of the night,
Filling the chilly room with perfume light. –
'And now, my love, my seraph fair, awake!
Thou art my heaven, and I thine eremite:
Open thine eyes, for meek St Agnes' sake,
Or I shall drowse beside thee, so my soul doth ache.'

Thus whispering, his warm, unnerved arm
Sank in her pillow. Shaded was her dream
By the dusk curtains: – 'twas a midnight charm
Impossible to melt as iced stream:
The lustrous salvers in the moonlight gleam;
Broad golden fringe upon the carpet lies:
It seem'd he never, never could redeem
From such a stedfast spell his lady's eyes;
So mus'd awhile, entoil'd in woofed phantasies.

Awakening up, he took her hollow lute, –
Tumultuous, – and, in chords that tenderest be,
He play'd an ancient ditty, long since mute,
In Provence call'd 'La belle dame sans mercy':
Close to her ear touching the melody: –
Wherewith disturb'd, she utter'd a soft moan:
He ceased – she panted quick – and suddenly
Her blue affrayed eyes wide open shone:
Upon his knees he sank, pale as smooth-sculptured stone.

Her eyes were open, but she still beheld,
Now wide awake, the vision of her sleep:
There was a painful change, that nigh expell'd
The blisses of her dream so pure and deep
At which fair Madeline began to weep,
And moan forth witless words with many a sigh;
While still her gaze on Porphyro would keep;
Who knelt, with joined hands and piteous eye,
Fearing to move or speak, she look'd so dreamingly.

'Ah, Porphyro!' said she, 'but even now
Thy voice was at sweet tremble in mine ear,
Made tuneable with every sweetest vow;
And those sad eyes were spiritual and clear:
How chang'd thou art! how pallid, chill, and drear!
Give me that voice again, my Porphyro,
Those looks immortal, those complainings dear!
Oh leave me not in this eternal woe,
For if thou diest, my Love, I know not where to go.'

Beyond a mortal man impassion'd far
At these voluptuous accents, he arose,
Ethereal, flush'd, and like a throbbing star
Seen mid the sapphire heaven's deep repose;
Into her dream he melted, as the rose
Blendeth its odour with the violet, –
Solution sweet: meantime the frost-wind blows
Like Love's alarum pattering the sharp sleet
Against the window-panes; St Agnes' moon hath set.

JOHN DONNE 1572–1631

THE DREAME

Deare love, for nothing lesse than thee
Would I have broke this happy dreame,
It was a theame
For reason, much too strong for phantasie,
Therefore thou wakd'st me wisely; yet
My Dreame thou brok'st not, but continued'st it,
Thou art so truth, that thoughts of thee suffice,
To make dreames truths; and fables histories;
Enter these armes, for since thou thoughtst it best,
Not to dreame all my dreame, let's act the rest.

As lightning, or a Tapers light,
Thine eyes, and not thy noise wak'd mee;
Yet I thought thee
(For thou lovest truth) an Angell, at first sight,
But when I saw thou sawest my heart,
And knew'st my thoughts, beyond an Angels art,
When thou knew'st what I dreamt, when thou knew'st when
Excesse of joy would wake me, and cam'st then,
I must confesse, it could not chuse but bee
Prophane, to think thee any thing but thee.

Comming and staying show'd thee, thee,
But rising makes me doubt, that now,
Thou art not thou.
That love is weake, where feare's as strong as hee;
'Tis not all spirit, pure, and brave,
If mixture it of *Feare*, *Shame*, *Honor*, have.
Perchance as torches which must ready bee,
Men light and put out, so thou deal'st with mee,
Thou cam'st to kindle, goest to come; Then I
Will dreame that hope againe, but else would die.

JOHN MILTON 1608–74

'METHOUGHT I SAW MY LATE ESPOUSED SAINT'

Methought I saw my late espousèd saint
  Brought to me like Alcestis from the grave,
  Whom Jove's great son to her glad husband gave,
  Rescued from death by force though pale and faint.
Mine as whom washed from spot of childbed taint,
  Purification in the old Law did save,
  And such, as yet once more I trust to have
  Full sight of her in Heaven without restraint,
Came vested all in white, pure as her mind:
  Her face was veiled, yet to my fancied sight,
  Love, sweetness, goodness, in her person shined
So clear, as in no face with more delight.
  But O as to embrace me she inclined
  I waked, she fled, and day brought back my night.

THOMAS HARDY 1840–1928

THE VOICE

Woman much missed, how you call to me, call to me,
Saying that now you are not as you were
When you had changed from the one who was all to me,
But as at first, when our day was fair.

Can it be you that I hear? Let me view you, then,
Standing as when I drew near to the town
Where you would wait for me: yes, as I knew you then,
Even to the original air-blue gown!

Or is it only the breeze, in its listlessness
Travelling across the wet mead to me here,
You being ever dissolved to wan wistlessness,
Heard no more again far or near?

    Thus I; faltering forward,
    Leaves around me falling,
Wind oozing thin through the thorn from norward,
    And the woman calling.

HUGO WILLIAMS 1942–

SIREN SONG

I phoned from time to time, to see if she's
changed the music on her answerphone.
'Tell me in two words,' goes the recording,
'what you were going to tell in a thousand.'

I peer into that thought, like peering out
to sea at night, hearing the sound of waves
breaking on rocks, knowing she is there,
listening, waiting for me to speak.

Once in a while she'll pick up the phone
and her voice sings to me out of the past.
The hair on the back of my neck stands up
as I catch her smell for a second.

SIR THOMAS WYATT 1503?–42

'THEY FLEE FROM ME'

They flee from me that sometime did me seek
  With naked foot stalking in my chamber.
I have seen them gentle tame and meek
  That now are wild and do not remember
  That sometime they put themselves in danger
To take bread at my hand; and now they range
Busily seeking with a continual change.

Thanked be fortune, it hath been otherwise
  Twenty times better; but once in special,
In thin array after a pleasant guise,
  When her loose gown from her shoulders did fall,
  And she me caught in her arms long and small;
And therewithal sweetly did me kiss,
And softly said, *Dear heart, how like you this?*

It was no dream, I lay broad waking.
  But all is turned thorough my gentleness
Into a strange fashion of forsaking;
  And I have leave to go of her goodness
  And she also to use newfangleness.
But since that I so kindely am served,
I would fain know what she hath deserved.

VICKI FEAVER 1943–

COAT

Sometimes I have wanted
to throw you off
like a heavy coat.

Sometimes I have said
you would not let me
breathe or move.

But now that I am free
to choose light clothes
or none at all

I feel the cold
and all the time I think
how warm it used to be.

EDWIN MORGAN 1920–

ONE CIGARETTE

No smoke without you, my fire.
After you left,
your cigarette glowed on in my ashtray
and sent up a long thread of such quiet grey
I smiled to wonder who would believe its signal
of so much love. One cigarette
in the non-smoker's tray.
As the last spire
trembles up, a sudden draught
blows it winding into my face.
Is it smell, is it taste?
You are here again, and I am drunk on your tobacco lips.
Out with the light.
Let the smoke lie back in the dark.
Till I hear the very ash
sigh down among the flowers of brass
I'll breathe, and long past midnight, your last kiss.

THOMAS HARDY 1840–1928

AFTER A JOURNEY

Hereto I come to view a voiceless ghost;
Whither, O whither will its whim now draw me?
Up the cliff, down, till I'm lonely, lost,
And the unseen waters' ejaculations awe me.
Where you will next be there's no knowing,
Facing round about me everywhere,
With your nut-coloured hair,
And gray eyes, and rose-flush coming and going.

Yes: I have re-entered your olden haunts at last;
Through the years, through the dead scenes I have tracked you
What have you now found to say of our past –
Scanned across the dark space wherein I have lacked you?
Summer gave us sweets, but autumn wrought division?
Things were not lastly as firstly well
With us twain, you tell?
But all's closed now, despite Time's derision.

I see what you are doing: you are leading me on
To the spots we knew when we haunted here together,
The waterfall, above which the mist-bow shone
At the then fair hour in the then fair weather,
And the cave just under, with a voice still so hollow
That it seems to call out to me from forty years ago,
When you were all aglow,
And not the thin ghost that I now frailly follow!

Ignorant of what there is flitting here to see,
    The waked birds preen and the seals flop lazily,
Soon you will have, Dear, to vanish from me,
    For the stars close their shutters and the dawn whitens hazily.
Trust me, I mind not, though Life lours,
    The bringing me here; nay, bring me here again!
        I am just the same as when
Our days were a joy, and our paths through flowers.

ALFRED, LORD TENNYSON 1809–92

from MAUD

O that 'twere possible
After long grief and pain
To find the arms of my true love
Round me once again!

When I was wont to meet her
In the silent woody places
By the home that gave me birth,
We stood tranced in long embraces
Mixt with kisses sweeter sweeter
Than anything on earth.

A shadow flits before me,
Not thou, but like to thee:
Ah Christ, that it were possible
For one short hour to see
The souls we loved, that they might tell us
What and where they be.

It leads me forth at evening,
It lightly winds and steals
In a cold white robe before me,
When all my spirit reels
As the shouts, the leagues of lights,
And the roaring of the wheels.

Half the night I waste in sighs,
Half in dreams I sorrow after
The delight of early skies;
In a wakeful doze I sorrow
For the hand, the lips, the eyes,
For the meeting of the morrow,

The delight of happy laughter,
The delight of low replies.

'Tis a morning pure and sweet,
And a dewy splendour falls
On the little flower that clings
To the turrets and the walls;
'Tis a morning pure and sweet,
And the light and shadow fleet;
She is walking in the meadow,
And the woodland echo rings;
In a moment we shall meet;
She is singing in the meadow
And the rivulet at her feet
Ripples on in light and shadow
To the ballad that she sings.

Do I hear her sing of old,
My bird with the shining head,
My own dove with the tender eye?
But there rings on a sudden a passionate cry,
There is some one dying or dead,
And a sullen thunder is rolled;
For a tumult shakes the city,
And I wake, my dream is fled;
In the shuddering dawn, behold,
Without knowledge, without pity,
By the curtains of my bed
That abiding phantom cold.

Get thee hence, nor come again,
Mix not memory with doubt,

Pass, thou deathlike type of pain,
Pass and cease to move about!
'Tis the blot upon the brain
That will show itself without.

Then I rise, the eavedrops fall,
And the yellow vapours choke
The great city sounding wide;
The day comes, a dull red ball
Wrapt in drifts of lurid smoke
On the misty river-tide.

Through the hubbub of the market
I steal, a wasted frame,
It crosses here, it crosses there,
Through all that crowd confused and loud,
The shadow still the same;
And on my heavy eyelids
My anguish hangs like shame.

Alas for her that met me,
That heard me softly call,
Came glimmering through the laurels
At the quiet evenfall,
In the garden by the turrets
Of the old manorial hall.

Would the happy spirit descend,
From the realms of light and song,
In the chamber or the street,
As she looks among the blest,

Should I fear to greet my friend,
Or to say 'Forgive the wrong,'
Or to ask her, 'Take me, sweet,
To the regions of thy rest'?

But the broad light glares and beats,
And the shadow flits and fleets
And will not let me be;
And I loathe the squares and streets,
And the faces that one meets,
Hearts with no love for me:
Always I long to creep
Into some still cavern deep,
There to weep, and weep, and weep
My whole soul out to thee.

ELIZABETH JENNINGS 1926–

ONE FLESH

Lying apart now, each in a separate bed,
He with a book, keeping the light on late,
She like a girl dreaming of childhood,
All men elsewhere – it is as if they wait
Some new event: the book he holds unread,
Her eyes fixed on the shadows overhead.

Tossed up like flotsam from a former passion,
How cool they lie. They hardly ever touch,
Or if they do it is like a confession
Of having little feeling – or too much.
Chastity faces them, a destination
For which their whole lives were a preparation.

Strangely apart, yet strangely together,
Silence between them like a thread to hold
And not wind in. And time itself's a feather
Touching them gently. Do they know they're old,
These two who are my father and my mother
Whose fire, from which I came, has now grown cold?

WILLIAM SHAKESPEARE 1564–1616

SONNET 302

Farewell! thou art too dear for my possessing,
And like enough thou know'st thy estimate:
The charter of thy worth gives thee releasing;
My bonds in thee are all determinate.
For how do I hold thee but by thy granting?
And for that riches where is my deserving?
The cause of this fair gift in me is wanting,
And so my patent back again is swerving.
Thyself thou gav'st, thy own worth then not knowing,
Or me, to whom thou gav'st it, else mistaking;
So thy great gift, upon misprision growing,
Comes home again, on better judgement making.
  Thus have I had thee, as a dream doth flatter,
  In sleep a king, but, waking, no such matter.

'There is no bliss like this'

STEVIE SMITH 1902–71

CONVICTION

I like to get off with people,
I like to lie in their arms,
I like to be held and tightly kissed,
Safe from all alarms.

I like to laugh and be happy
With a beautiful beautiful kiss,
I tell you, in all the world
There is no bliss like this.

JOHN DRYDEN 1631–1700

SONG

After the pangs of a desperate lover,
When day and night I have sighed all in vain,
Ah what a pleasure it is to discover
In her eyes pity, who causes my pain!

When with unkindness our love at a stand is,
And both have punished ourselves with the pain,
Ah what a pleasure the touch of her hand is,
Ah what a pleasure to press it again!

When the denial comes fainter and fainter,
And her eyes give what her tongue does deny,
Ah what a trembling I feel when I venture,
Ah what a trembling does usher my joy!

When with a sigh she accords me the blessing,
And her eyes twinkle 'twixt pleasure and pain,
Ah what a joy 'tis beyond all expressing,
Ah what a joy to hear, 'shall we again?'!

E.E. CUMMINGS 1894–1962

MAY I FEEL

may i feel said he
(i'll squeal said she
just once said he)
it's fun said she

(may i touch said he
how much said she
a lot said he)
why not said she

(let's go said he
not too far said she
what's too far said he
where you are said she)

may i stay said he
(which way said she
like this said he
if you kiss said she

may i move said he
is it love said she)
if you're willing said he
(but you're killing said she

but it's life said he
but your wife said she
now said he)
ow said she

(tiptop said he
don't stop said she
oh no said he)
go slow said she

(cccome?said he
ummm said she)
you're divine!said he
(you are Mine said she)

CHARLES BAUDELAIRE 1821–67

THE JEWELS

translated by ROY CAMPBELL

My well-beloved was stripped. Knowing my whim,
She wore her tinkling gems, but naught besides:
And showed such pride as, while her luck betides,
A sultan's favoured slave may show to him.

When it lets off its lively, crackling sound,
This blazing blend of metal crossed with stone,
Gives me an ecstasy I've only known
Where league of sound and lustre can be found.

She let herself be loved: then, drowsy-eyed,
Smiled down from her high couch in languid ease.
My love was deep and gentle as the seas
And rose to her as to a cliff the tide.

My own approval of each dreamy pose,
Like a tamed tiger, cunningly she sighted:
And candour, with lubricity united,
Gave piquancy to every one she chose.

Her limbs and hips, burnished with changing lustres,
Before my eyes clairvoyant and serene,
Swanned themselves, undulating in their sheen;
Her breasts and belly, of my vine the clusters,

Like evil angels rose, my fancy twitting,
To kill the peace which over me she'd thrown,
And to disturb her from the crystal throne
Where, calm and solitary, she was sitting.

So swerved her pelvis that, in one design,
Antiope's white rump it seemed to graft
To a boy's torso, merging fore and aft.
The talc on her brown tan seemed half-divine.

The lamp resigned its dying flame. Within,
The hearth alone lit up the darkened air,
And every time it sighed a crimson flare
It drowned in blood that amber-coloured skin.

CHRISTOPHER MARLOWE 1564–93

TRANSLATION OF *OVID, AMORES*

Book One, V

In summer's heat, and mid-time of the day,
To rest my limbs upon a bed I lay;
One window shut, the other open stood,
Which gave such light as twinkles in a wood,
Like twilight glimpse at setting of the sun,
Or night being past, and yet not day begun;
Such light to shamefaced maidens must be shown,
Where they may sport, and seem to be unknown:
Then came Corinna in a long loose gown,
Her white neck hid with tresses hanging down,
Resembling fair Semiramis going to bed,
Or Lais of a thousand wooers sped.
I snatched her gown: being thin, the harm was small,
Yet strived she to be covered therewithal;
And striving thus, as one that would be cast,
Betrayed herself, and yielded at the last.
Stark naked as she stood before mine eye,
Not one wen in her body could I spy.
What arms and shoulders did I touch and see!
How apt her breasts were to be pressed by me!
How smooth a belly under her waist saw I,
How large a leg, and what a lusty thigh!
To leave the rest, all liked me passing well;
I clinged her naked body, down she fell:
Judge you the rest: being tired she bade me kiss;
Jove send me more such afternoons as this.

WILLIAM CARLOS WILLIAMS 1883–1963

QUEEN-ANNE'S-LACE

Her body is not so white as
anemone petals nor so smooth – nor
so remote a thing. It is a field
of the wild carrot taking
the field by force; the grass
does not raise above it.
Here is no question of whiteness,
white as can be, with a purple mole
at the center of each flower.
Each flower is a hand's span
of her whiteness. Wherever
his hand has lain there is
a tiny purple blemish. Each part
is a blossom under his touch
to which the fibres of her being
stem one by one, each to its end,
until the whole field is a
white desire, empty, a single stem,
a cluster, flower by flower,
a pious wish to whiteness gone over –
or nothing.

DAVID HARTNETT 1952–

THE FLEECE

We went to the hovel of the midnight shearer
And lay together, naked, on a wooden board.
Swiftly his sharp-toothed comb skimmed and whirred
Peeling back the fleece our love had grown
Until it dropped away, limp in the straw,
Still warm from us, a loosened milky gown,
Though brambles snagged and blood-spots dabbed the wool.
I saw him knead its softness to a roll.
Then through wicket gates to a dark field
Weightless, we ran and lay together, numb.
Prickling stars of sweat our skins bristled
Until, wherever limb brushed against limb,
A luminous froth uncurled, shivered into flame.
By dawn what fleece had clothed us, new or old?

AUDRE LORDE 1934–92

ON A NIGHT OF THE FULL MOON

i

Out of my flesh that hungers
and my mouth that knows
comes the shape I am seeking
for reason.
The curve of your waiting body
fits my waiting hand
your breasts warm as sunlight
your lips as quick as young birds
between your thighs the sweet
sharp taste of limes.

Thus I hold you
frank in my heart's eye
in my skin's knowing
as my fingers conceive your flesh
I feel your stomach
moving against me.

Before the moon wanes again
we shall come together.

ii

And I would be the moon
spoken over your beckoning flesh
breaking against reservations
beaching thought
my hands at your high tide
over and under inside you
and the passing of hungers
attended, forgotten.

    Darkly risen
    the moon speaks
    my eyes
    judging your roundness
    delightful.

TED HUGHES 1930–98

LOVESONG

He loved her and she loved him
His kisses sucked out her whole past and future or tried to
He had no other appetite
She bit him she gnawed him she sucked
She wanted him complete inside her
Safe and sure forever and ever
Their little cries fluttered into the curtains

Her eyes wanted nothing to get away
Her looks nailed down his hands his wrists his elbows
He gripped her hard so that life
Should not drag her from that moment
He wanted all future to cease
He wanted to topple with his arms round her
Off that moment's brink and into nothing
Or everlasting or whatever there was
Her embrace was an immense press
To print him into her bones
His smiles were the garrets of a fairy palace
Where the real world would never come
Her smiles were spider bites
So he would lie still till she felt hungry
His words were occupying armies
Her laughs were an assassin's attempts
His looks were bullets daggers of revenge
Her glances were ghosts in the corner with horrible secrets
His whispers were whips and jackboots
Her kisses were lawyers steadily writing
His caresses were the last hooks of a castaway
Her love-tricks were the grinding of locks
And their deep cries crawled over the floors
Like an animal dragging a great trap
His promises were the surgeon's gag
Her promises took the top off his skull

She would get a brooch made of it
His vows pulled out all her sinews
He showed her how to make a love-knot
Her vows put his eyes in formalin
At the back of her secret drawer
Their screams stuck in the wall

Their heads fell apart into sleep like the two halves
Of a lopped melon, but love is hard to stop

In their entwined sleep they exchanged arms and legs
In their dreams their brains took each other hostage

In the morning they wore each other's face

MEDBH MCGUCKIAN 1950–

THE TIME BEFORE YOU

The secret of movement
Is not the secret itself
But the movement
Of there being a secret.

For example, the movement
Of an accordion, which closes
On one side and opens
On the other.

Or your folding one arm
Against your pushing body
At the turn towards waking
Which is the full length

Of your dream. When
You look at me as a man
May look, it is like a break
Of real sky where one branch

Crosses its fellow, a brown leaf
Taking September into
A brown stone, or green
Under green, grass below trees.

You ask the difference
Between a green shadow
And a brown one? Here
Is a green answer.

I can only say
I feel that green shadow,
That short, morning shadow,
Through and through me,

With a sense of hair in a coil
Recoiling from the fingers
That held it, smoothing
Its darkness till it would seem

Like whatever it is furthest
From, one of those blonde
Napes velvety as leaves
With the tip pointed towards you.

By now you will have painted
The first of the sea fresh staring
Yellow and changed its name.
So that now I always hear

The sea in the wind, though
I like a wind in which
You hear the rain, however moist
With breath its mask may be.

And after last night's rain
I actually dreamed of you,
Falling asleep for that
Wild purpose, seeing

Your face through the floor
As all the light left
On the flat of a hand.
I wish they could hear

That we lived in one room
And littered a new poetry
Long after both doors, up
And downstairs, shut.

A.C. SWINBURNE 1837–1909

LOVE AND SLEEP

Lying asleep between the strokes of night
I saw my love lean over my sad bed,
Pale as the duskiest lily's leaf or head,
Smooth-skinned and dark, with bare throat made to bite,
Too wan for blushing and too warm for white,
But perfect-coloured without white or red.
And her lips opened amorously, and said –
I wist not what, saving one word – Delight.
And all her face was honey to my mouth,
And all her body pasture to mine eyes;
The long lithe arms and hotter hands than fire,
The quivering flanks, hair smelling of the south,
The bright light feet, the splendid supple thighs
And glittering eyelids of my soul's desire.

EDGELL RICKWORD 1898–1982

INTIMACY

Since I have seen you do those intimate things
that other men but dream of; lull asleep
the sinister dark forest of your hair
and tie the bows that stir on your calm breast
faintly as leaves that shudder in their sleep;
since I have seen your stocking swallow up,
a swift black wind, the flame of your pale foot,
and deemed your slender limbs so meshed in silk
sweet mermaid sisters drowned in their dark hair;
I have not troubled overmuch with food,
and wine has seemed like water from a well;
pavements are built of fire, grass of thin flames;
all other girls grow dull as painted flowers,
or flutter harmlessly like coloured flies
whose wings are tangled in the net of leaves
spread by frail trees that grow behind the eyes.

SHARON OLDS 1942–

MAKING LOVE

You wake up, and you do not know
where you are, or who you are
or what you are, the last light of the evening
coming up to the panes, not coming in,
the solid, slanted body of the desk
between the windows, its bird's-eye slightly
shining, here and there, in the wood. And you
try to think back, you cannot remember it,
it stands behind your mind, like a mountain,
at night, behind you, your pants are torn
or across the room or still dangling from one leg
like a heavy scarlet loop of the body, your
bra is half on or not on or you were naked to begin with,
you cannot remember, everything is changed.
Tomorrow, maybe, taking a child to school,
your foot in the air half off the curb you'll
see his mouth where it was and feel it and the
large double star of your two bodies,
but for now you are like the one in the crib,
you are everyone, right now,
the milky, greenish windows still as
sentinels, saying, *Don't worry,*
you will not remember, you will never know.

JOHN DONNE 1572–1631

THE SUNNE RISING

Busie old foole, unruly Sunne,
Why dost thou thus,
Through windowes, and through curtaines call on us?
Must to thy motions lovers seasons run?
Sawcy pedantique wretch, goe chide
Late schoole boyes, and sowre prentices,
Goe tell Court-huntsmen, that the King will ride,
Call countrey ants to harvest offices;
Love, all alike, no season knowes, nor clyme,
Nor houres, dayes, months, which are the rags of time.

Thy beames, so reverend, and strong
Why shouldst thou thinke?
I could eclipse and cloud them with a winke,
But that I would not lose her sight so long:
If her eyes have not blinded thine,
Looke, and to morrow late, tell mee,
Whether both the'India's of spice and Myne
Be where thou lefst them, or lie here with mee.
Aske for those Kings whom thou saw'st yesterday,
And thou shalt heare, All here in one bed lay.

She'is all States, and all Princes, I,
Nothing else is.
Princes doe but play us; compar'd to this,
All honor's mimique; All wealth alchimie.
Thou sunne art halfe as happy'as wee,
In that the world's contracted thus;
Thine age askes ease, and since thy duties bee
To warme the world, that's done in warming us.
Shine here to us, and thou art every where;
This bed thy center is, these walls, thy spheare.

JO SHAPCOTT 1953–

MUSE

When I kiss you in all the folding places
of your body, you make that noise like a dog
dreaming, dreaming of the long run he makes
in answer to some jolt to his hormones,
running across landfills, running, running
by tips and shorelines from the scent of too much,
but still going with head up and snout
in the air because he loves it all
and has to get away. I have to kiss deeper
and more slowly – your neck, your inner arm,
the neat creases under your toes, the shadow
behind your knee, the white angles of your groin –
until you fall quiet because only then
can I get the damned words to come into my mouth.

EDWIN MORGAN 1920–

STRAWBERRIES

There were never strawberries
like the ones we had
that sultry afternoon
sitting on the step
of the open french window
facing each other
your knees held in mine
the blue plates in our laps
the strawberries glistening
in the hot sunlight
we dipped them in sugar
looking at each other
not hurrying the feast
for one to come
the empty plates
laid on the stone together
with the two forks crossed
and I bent towards you
sweet in that air
in my arms
abandoned like a child
from your eager mouth
the taste of strawberries
in my memory
lean back again
let me love you

let the sun beat
on our forgetfulness
one hour of all
the heat intense
and summer lightning
on the Kilpatrick hills

let the storm wash the plates

'Th' expense of spirit in a waste of shame'

WILLIAM SHAKESPEARE 1564–1616

SONNET 129

Th' expense of spirit in a waste of shame
Is lust in action; and till action, lust
Is perjured, murderous, bloody, full of blame,
Savage, extreme, rude, cruel, not to trust;
Enjoyed no sooner but despisèd straight:
Past reason hunted; and no sooner had,
Past reason hated, as a swallowed bait,
On purpose laid to make the taker mad:
Mad in pursuit, and in possession so;
Had, having, and in quest to have, extreme;
A bliss in proof, and proved, a very woe;
Before, a joy proposed; behind, a dream.
  All this the world well knows; yet none knows well
  To shun the heaven that leads men to this hell.

ROBERT GRAVES 1895–1985

SYMPTOMS OF LOVE

Love is a universal migraine,
A bright stain on the vision
Blotting out reason.

Symptoms of true love
Are leanness, jealousy,
Laggard dawns;

Are omens and nightmares –
Listening for a knock,
Waiting for a sign

For a touch of her fingers
In a darkened room,
For a searching look.

Take courage, lover!
Can you endure such grief
At any hand but hers?

BEN JONSON 1572–1637

PETRONIUS ARBITER

translated from the Latin

Doing, a filthy pleasure is, and short;
And done, we straight repent us of the sport:
Let us not then rush blindly on unto it,
Like lustful beasts, that only know to do it:
For lust will languish, and that heat decay.
But thus, thus, keeping endless holiday,
Let us together closely lie and kiss,
There is no labour, nor no shame in this;
This hath pleased, doth please, and long will please; never
Can this decay, but is beginning ever.

W.B. YEATS 1865–1939

LEDA AND THE SWAN

A sudden blow: the great wings beating still
Above the staggering girl, her thighs caressed
By the dark webs, her nape caught in his bill,
He holds her helpless breast upon his breast.

How can those terrified vague fingers push
The feathered glory from her loosening thighs?
And how can body, laid in that white rush,
But feel the strange heart beating where it lies?

A shudder in the loins engenders there
The broken wall, the burning roof and tower
And Agamemnon dead.
                                        Being so caught up,
So mastered by the brute blood of the air,
Did she put on his knowledge with his power
Before the indifferent beak could let her drop?

A.C. SWINBURNE 1837–1909

BEFORE PARTING

A month or twain to live on honeycomb
Is pleasant; but one tires of scented time,
Cold sweet recurrence of accepted rhyme,
And that strong purple under juice and foam
Where the wine's heart has burst;
Nor feel the latter kisses like the first.

Once yet, this poor one time; I will not pray
Even to change the bitterness of it,
The bitter taste ensuring on the sweet,
To make your tears fall where your soft hair lay
All blurred and heavy in some perfumed wise
Over my face and eyes.

And yet who knows what end the scythèd wheat
Makes of its foolish poppies' mouths of red?
These were not sown, these are not harvested,
They grow a month and are cast under feet
And none has care thereof,
As none has care of a divided love.

I know each shadow of your lips by rote,
Each change of love in eyelids and eyebrows;
The fashion of fair temples tremulous
With tender blood, and colour of your throat;
I know not how love is gone out of this,
Seeing that all was his.

Love's likeness there endures upon all these:
But out of these one shall not gather love.
Day hath not strength nor the night shade enough
To make love whole and fill his lips with ease,
As some bee-builded cell
Feels at filled lips the heavy honey swell.

I know not how this last month leaves your hair
Less full of purple colour and hid spice,
And that luxurious trouble of closed eyes
Is mixed with meaner shadow and waste care;
And love, kissed out by pleasure, seems not yet
Worth patience to regret.

EDNA ST VINCENT MILLAY 1892–1950

[SONNET]

I, being born a woman and distressed
By all the needs and notions of my kind,
Am urged by your propinquity to find
Your person fair, and feel a certain zest
To bear your body's weight upon my breast:
So subtly is the fume of life designed,
To clarify the pulse and cloud the mind,
And leave me once again undone, possessed.
Think not for this, however, the poor treason
Of my stout blood against my staggering brain,
I shall remember you with love, or season
My scorn with pity, – let me make it plain:
I find this frenzy insufficient reason
For conversation when we meet again.

D.H. LAWRENCE 1885–1930

DESIRE

Ah, in the past, towards rare individuals
I have felt the pull of desire:
Oh come, come nearer, come into touch!
Come physically nearer, be flesh to my flesh –

But say little, oh say little,
and afterwards, leave me alone.
Keep your aloneness, leave me my aloneness. –
I used to say this, in the past – but now no more.
It has always been a failure.
They have always insisted on love
and on talking about it
and on the me-and-thee and what we meant to each other.

So now I have no desire any more
Except to be left, in the last resort, alone, quite alone.

'is there Beauty yet to find?'

JOHN KEATS 1795–1821

ODE TO A NIGHTINGALE

1

My heart aches, and a drowsy numbness pains
My sense, as though of hemlock I had drunk,
Or emptied some dull opiate to the drains
One minute past, and Lethe-wards had sunk:
'Tis not through envy of thy happy lot,
But being too happy in thine happiness—
That thou, light-wingéd Dryad of the trees,
In some melodious plot
Of beechen green, and shadows numberless,
Singest of summer in full-throated ease.

2

O, for a draught of vintage! that hath been
Cooled a long age in the deep-delvéd earth,
Tasting of Flora and the country green,
Dance, and Provençal song, and sunburnt mirth!
O for a beaker full of the warm South,
Full of the true, the blushful Hippocrene,
With beaded bubbles winking at the brim,
And purple-stainéd mouth;
That I might drink, and leave the world unseen,
And with thee fade away into the forest dim:

3

Fade far away, dissolve, and quite forget
What thou among the leaves has never known,
The weariness, the fever, and the fret
Here, where men sit and hear each other groan;

Where palsy shakes a few, sad, last gray hairs,
  Where youth grows pale, and specter-thin, and dies,
    Where but to think is to be full of sorrow
      And leaden-eyed despairs,
  Where Beauty cannot keep her lustrous eyes,
    Or new Love pine at them beyond tomorrow.

4

Away! away! for I will fly to thee,
  Not charioted by Bacchus and his pards,
But on the viewless wings of Poesy,
  Though the dull brain perplexes and retards:
Already with thee! tender is the night,
  And haply the Queen-Moon is on her throne,
    Clustered around by all her starry Fays;
      But here there is no light,
  Save what from heaven is with the breezes blown
    Through verdurous glooms and winding mossy ways.

5

I cannot see what flowers are at my feet,
  Nor what soft incense hangs upon the boughs,
But, in embalméd darkness, guess each sweet
  Wherewith the seasonable month endows
The grass, the thicket, and the fruit tree wild;
  White hawthorn, and the pastoral eglantine;
    Fast fading violets covered up in leaves;
      And mid-May's eldest child,
  The coming musk-rose, full of dewy wine,
    The murmurous haunt of flies on summer eves.

6

Darkling I listen; and for many a time
  I have been half in love with easeful Death,

Called him soft names in many a muséd rhyme,
To take into the air my quiet breath;
Now more than ever seems it rich to die,
To cease upon the midnight with no pain,
While thou art pouring forth thy soul abroad
In such an ecstasy!
Still wouldst thou sing, and I have ears in vain—
To thy high requiem become a sod.

7

Thou wast not born for death, immortal Bird!
No hungry generations tread thee down;
The voice I hear this passing night was heard
In ancient days by emperor and clown:
Perhaps the selfsame song that found a path
Through the sad heart of Ruth, when, sick for home,
She stood in tears amid the alien corn;
The same that ofttimes hath
Charmed magic casements, opening on the foam
Of perilous seas, in faery lands forlorn.

8

Forlorn! the very word is like a bell
To toll me back from thee to my sole self!
Adieu! the fancy cannot cheat so well
As she is famed to do, deceiving elf.
Adieu! adieu! thy plaintive anthem fades
Past the near meadows, over the still stream,
Up the hill side; and now 'tis buried deep
In the next valley-glades:
Was it a vision, or a waking dream?
Fled is that music:—Do I wake or sleep?

ROBERT BROWNING 1812–89

HOME-THOUGHTS, FROM ABROAD

I

Oh, to be in England
Now that April's there,
And whoever wakes in England
Sees, some morning, unaware,
That the lowest boughs and the brushwood sheaf
Round the elm-tree bole are in tiny leaf,
While the chaffinch sings on the orchard bough
In England – now!

II

And after April, when May follows,
And the whitethroat builds, and all the swallows!
Hark, where my blossomed pear-tree in the hedge
Leans to the field and scatters on the clover
Blossoms and dewdrops – at the bent spray's edge –
That's the wise thrush; he sings each song twice over,
Lest you should think he never could recapture
The first fine careless rapture!
And though the fields look rough with hoary dew
All will be gay when noontide wakes anew
The buttercups, the little children's dower
– Far brighter than this gaudy melon-flower!

PERCY BYSSHE SHELLEY 1792–1822

TO A SKYLARK

Hail to thee, blithe Spirit!
Bird thou never wert,
That from Heaven, or near it,
Pourest thy full heart
In profuse strains of unpremeditated art.

Higher still and higher
From the earth thou springest
Like a cloud of fire;
The blue deep thou wingest,
And singing still dost soar, and soaring ever singest.

In the golden lightning
Of the sunken sun,
O'er which clouds are bright'ning,
Thou dost float and run;
Like an unbodied joy whose race is just begun.

The pale purple even
Melts around thy flight;
Like a star of Heaven,
In the broad daylight
Thou art unseen, but yet I hear thy shrill delight,

Keen as are the arrows
Of that silver sphere,
Whose intense lamp narrows
In the white dawn clear
Until we hardly see—we feel that it is there.

All the earth and air
With thy voice is loud,
As, when night is bare,
From one lonely cloud
The moon rains out her beams, and Heaven is overflowed.

What thou art we know not;
What is most like thee?
From rainbow clouds there flow not
Drops so bright to see
As from thy presence showers a rain of melody.

Like a Poet hidden
In the light of thought,
Singing hymns unbidden,
Till the world is wrought
To sympathy with hopes and fears it heeded not:

Like a high-born maiden
In a palace tower,
Soothing her love-laden
Soul in secret hour
With music sweet as love, which overflows her bower:

Like a glowworm golden
In a dell of dew,
Scattering unbeholden
Its aërial hue
Among the flowers and grass, which screen it from the view!

Like a rose embowered
In its own green leaves,
By warm winds deflowered,
Till the scent it gives
Makes faint with too much sweet those heavy-wingéd thieves:

Sound of vernal showers
On the twinkling grass,
Rain-awakened flowers,
All that ever was
Joyous, and clear, and fresh, thy music doth surpass:

Teach us, Sprite or Bird,
What sweet thoughts are thine:
I have never heard
Praise of love or wine
That panted forth a flood of rapture so divine.

Chorus Hymeneal,
Or triumphal chant,
Matched with thine would be all
But an empty vaunt,
A thing wherein we feel there is some hidden want.

What objects are the fountains
Of thy happy strain?
What fields, or waves, or mountains?
What shapes of sky or plain?
What love of thine own kind? what ignorance of pain?

Why thy clear keen joyance
Languor cannot be:
Shadow of annoyance
Never came near thee:
Thou lovest—but ne'er knew love's sad satiety.

Waking or asleep,
Thou of death must deem
Things more true and deep
Than we mortals dream,
Or how could thy notes flow in such a crystal stream?

We look before and after,
And pine for what is not:
Our sincerest laughter
With some pain is fraught;
Our sweetest songs are those that tell of saddest thought.

Yet if we could scorn
Hate, and pride, and fear;
If we were things born
Not to shed a tear,
I know not how thy joy we ever should come near.

Better than all measures
Of delightful sound,
Better than all treasures
That in books are found,
Thy skill to poet were, thou scorner of the ground!

Teach me half the gladness
That thy brain must know,
Such harmonious madness
From my lips would flow
The world should listen then—as I am listening now.

JOHN CLARE 1793–1864

SABBATH BELLS

Ive often on a sabbath day
Where pastoral quiet dwells
Lay down among the new mown hay
To listen distant bells
That beautifully flung the sound
Upon the quiet wind
While beans in blossom breathed around
A fragrance oer the mind

A fragrance and a joy beside
That never wears away
The very air seems deified
Upon a sabbath day
So beautiful the flitting wrack
Slow pausing from the eye
Earths music seemed to call them back
Calm settled in the sky

And I have listened till I felt
A feeling not in words
A love that rudest moods would melt
When those sweet sounds was heard
A melancholly joy at rest
A pleasurable pain
A love a rapture of the breast
That nothing will explain

A dream of beauty that displays
Imaginary joys
That all the world in all its ways
Finds not to realize
All idly stretched upon the hay
The wind flirt fanning bye
How soft how sweetly swept away
The music of the sky

The ear it lost and caught the sound
Swelled beautifully on
A fitful melody around
Of sweetness heard and gone
I felt such thoughts I yearned to sing
The humming airs delight
That seemed to move the swallows wing
Into a wilder flight

The butterflye in wings of brown
Would find me where I lay
Fluttering and bobbing up and down
And settling on the hay
The waving blossoms seemed to throw
Their fragrance to the sound
While up and down and loud and low
The bells were ringing round

RUPERT BROOKE 1887–1915

from THE OLD VICARAGE, GRANTCHESTER

Ah God! to see the branches stir
Across the moon at Grantchester!
To smell the thrilling-sweet and rotten
Unforgettable, unforgotten
River-smell, and hear the breeze
Sobbing in the little trees.
Say, do the elm-clumps greatly stand
Still guardians of that holy land?
The chestnuts shade, in reverend dream,
The yet unacademic stream?
Is dawn a secret shy and cold
Anadyomene, silver-gold?
And sunset still a golden sea
From Haslingfield to Madingley?
And after, ere the night is born,
Do hares come out about the corn?
Oh, is the water sweet and cool,
Gentle and brown, above the pool?
And laughs the immortal river still
Under the mill, under the mill?
Say, is there Beauty yet to find?
And Certainty? and Quiet kind?
Deep meadows yet, for to forget
The lies, and truths, and pain? . . . Oh! yet
Stands the Church clock at ten to three?
And is there honey still for tea?

ELIZABETH DARYUSH 1887–1977

STILL-LIFE

Through the open French window the warm sun
lights up the polished breakfast-table, laid
round a bowl of crimson roses, for one –
a service of Worcester porcelain, arrayed
near it a melon, peaches, figs, small hot
rolls in a napkin, fairy rack of toast,
butter in ice, high silver coffee pot,
and, heaped on a salver, the morning's post.

She comes over the lawn, the young heiress,
from her early walk in her garden-wood,
feeling that life's a table set to bless
her delicate desires with all that's good,

that even the unopened future lies
like a love-letter, full of sweet surprise.

ELIZABETH GARRETT 1958–

MOULES A LA MARINIERE

We scoured the secret places of the creek,
Parting blistered fronds of bladder-wrack
To find the concupiscent clusters, rocked
In their granite crêche. Jack-knives prised
The molluscs out. Slick blue-blacks bruised
Slowly dull; and the sea expunged our tracks.

Bouquet of Muscadet, bouquet garni recall
The tuck and chuckle of mussels in a bucket
Behind the door. Damp and aromatic,
Steam insinuates itself into all
The kitchen clefts, and clings in briny beads
Above the flame where mussels chirp and wheeze.

I pour on wine; it seems they beg for more,
The beaked shells yearning wide as if in song –
Yet dumb – and lewdly lolling parrot-tongues.
Cream licks the back of a spoon and drawls a slur
Of unctuous benediction for this feast.
We smooth our cassocks; bow our heads; and eat.

It rained all night as though to wash away
A brininess that tanged the atmosphere:
Dreams – of forbidden fruit, of *fruits de mer*
Wrenched from their secret beds, of tastes that lay
Like sea's after-sting on the tongue. Still lingers
A trace of guilt. I wash my salty fingers.

MAY SWENSON 1919–

THE CENTAUR

The summer that I was ten –
Can it be there was only one
summer that I was ten? It must

have been a long one then –
each day I'd go out to choose
a fresh horse from my stable

which was a willow grove
down by the old canal.
I'd go on my two bare feet.

But when, with my brother's jack-knife,
I had cut me a long limber horse
with a good thick knob for a head,

and peeled him slick and clean
except a few leaves for the tail,
and cinched my brother's belt

around his head for a rein,
I'd straddle and canter him fast
up the grass bank to the path,

trot along in the lovely dust
that talcumed over his hoofs,
hiding my toes, and turning

his feet to swift half-moons.
The willow knob with the strap
jouncing between my thighs

was the pommel and yet the poll
of my nickering pony's head.
My head and my neck were mine,

yet they were shaped like a horse.
My hair flopped to the side
like the mane of a horse in the wind.

My forelock swung in my eyes,
my neck arched and I snorted.
I shied and skittered and reared,

stopped and raised my knees,
pawed at the ground and quivered.
My teeth bared as we wheeled

and swished through the dust again.
I was the horse and the rider,
and the leather I slapped to his rump

spanked my own behind.
Doubled, my two hoofs beat
a gallop along the bank,

the wind twanged in my mane,
my mouth squared to the bit.
And yet I sat on my steed

quiet, negligent riding,
my toes standing the stirrups,
my thighs hugging his ribs.

At a walk we drew up to the porch.
I tethered him to a paling.
Dismounting, I smoothed my skirt

and entered the dusky hall.
My feet on the clean linoleum
left ghostly toes in the hall.

Where have you been? said my mother.
Been riding, I said from the sink,
and filled me a glass of water.

What's that in your pocket? she said.
Just my knife. It weighted my pocket
and stretched my dress awry.

Go tie back your hair, said my mother,
and *Why is your mouth all green?*
Rob Roy, he pulled some clover
as we crossed the field, I told her.

ROY CAMPBELL 1901–57

THE SISTERS

After hot loveless nights, when cold winds stream
Sprinkling the frost and dew, before the light,
Bored with the foolish things that girls must dream
Because their beds are empty of delight,

Two sisters rise and strip. Out from the night
Their horses run to their low-whistled pleas –
Vast phantom shapes with eyeballs rolling white
That sneeze a fiery stream about their knees:

Through the crisp manes their stealthy prowling hands,
Stronger than curbs, in slow caresses rove,
They gallop down across the milk-white sands
And wade far out into the sleeping cove:

The frost stings sweetly with a burning kiss
As intimate as love, as cold as death:
Their lips, whereon delicious tremors hiss,
Fume with the ghostly pollen of their breath.

Far out on the grey silence of the flood
They watch the dawn in smouldering gyres expand
Beyond them: and the day burns through their blood
Like a white candle through a shuttered hand.

ALFRED, LORD TENNYSON 1809–92

ULYSSES

It little profits that an idle king,
By this still hearth, among these barren crags,
Matched with an aged wife, I mete and dole
Unequal laws unto a savage race,
That hoard, and sleep, and feed, and know not me.

I cannot rest from travel: I will drink
Life to the lees: all times I have enjoyed
Greatly, have suffered greatly, both with those
That loved me, and alone; on shore, and when
Through scudding drifts the rainy Hyades
Vext the dim sea: I am become a name;
For always roaming with a hungry heart
Much have I seen and known; cities of men
And manners, climates, councils, governments,
Myself not least, but honoured of them all;
And drunk delight of battle with my peers,
Far on the ringing plains of windy Troy.
I am a part of all that I have met;
Yet all experience is an arch wherethrough
Gleams that untravelled world whose margin fades
For ever and for ever when I move.
How dull it is to pause, to make an end,
To rust unburnished, not to shine in use!
As though to breathe were life! Life piled on life
Were all too little, and of one to me
Little remains: but every hour is saved
From that eternal silence, something more,
A bringer of new things; and vile it were
For some three suns to store and hoard myself,
And this grey spirit yearning in desire
To follow knowledge like a sinking star,
Beyond the utmost bound of human thought.

This is my son, mine own Telemachus,
To whom I leave the sceptre and the isle—
Well-loved of me, discerning to fulfil
This labour, by slow prudence to make mild
A rugged people, and through soft degrees
Subdue them to the useful and the good.
Most blameless is he, centred in the sphere
Of common duties, decent not to fail
In offices of tenderness, and pay
Meet adoration to my household gods,
When I am gone. He works his work, I mine.

There lies the port; the vessel puffs her sail:
There gloom the dark, broad seas. My mariners,
Souls that have toiled, and wrought, and thought with me—
That ever with a frolic welcome took
The thunder and the sunshine, and opposed
Free hearts, free foreheads—you and I are old;
Old age hath yet his honour and his toil;
Death closes all: but something ere the end,
Some work of noble note, may yet be done,
Not unbecoming men that strove with Gods.
The lights begin to twinkle from the rocks:
The long day wanes: the slow moon climbs: the deep
Moans round with many voices. Come, my friends,
'Tis not too late to seek a newer world.
Push off, and sitting well in order smite
The sounding furrows; for my purpose holds
To sail beyond the sunset, and the baths
Of all the western stars, until I die.
It may be that the gulfs will wash us down:
It may be we shall touch the Happy Isles,
And see the great Achilles, whom we knew.

Though much is taken, much abides; and though
We are not now that strength which in old days
Moved earth and heaven; that which we are, we are,
One equal temper of heroic hearts,
Made weak by time and fate, but strong in will
To strive, to seek, to find, and not to yield.

JOHN KEATS 1795–1821

TO AUTUMN

1

Season of mists and mellow fruitfulness,
Close bosom-friend of the maturing sun;
Conspiring with him how to load and bless
With fruit the vines that round the thatch-eaves run;
To bend with apples the mossed cottage-trees,
And fill all fruit with ripeness to the core;
To swell the gourd, and plump the hazel shells
With a sweet kernel; to set budding more,
And still more, later flowers for the bees,
Until they think warm days will never cease,
For Summer has o'er-brimmed their clammy cells.

2

Who hath not seen thee oft amid thy store?
Sometimes whoever seeks abroad may find
Thee sitting careless on a granary floor,
Thy hair soft-lifted by the winnowing wind;
Or on a half-reaped furrow sound asleep,
Drowsed with the fume of poppies, while thy hook
Spares the next swath and all its twinéd flowers:
And sometimes like a gleaner thou dost keep
Steady thy laden head across a brook;
Or by a cider-press, with patient look,
Thou watchest the last oozings hours by hours.

3

Where are the songs of Spring? Aye, where are they?
Think not of them, thou hast thy music too—
While barréd clouds bloom the soft-dying day,
And touch the stubble-plains with rosy hue;
Then in a wailful choir the small gnats mourn
Among the river sallows, borne aloft
Or sinking as the light wind lives or dies;

And full-grown lambs loud bleat from hilly bourn;
  Hedge crickets sing; and now with treble soft
The redbreast whistles from a garden-croft;
  And gathering swallows twitter in the skies.

ACKNOWLEDGEMENTS

— ◇ —

The publishers would like to make the following acknowledgements for permission to reproduce copyright material. Every effort has been made to trace copyright holders but in a few cases this has proved imposssible. The publishers would be interested to hear from any copyright holders not here acknowledged.

15, 44. Poems 249 □Wild Nights — Wild Nights!□ and 315 □He fumbles at your Soul□ by Emily Dickinson are reprinted by permission of the publishers and the Trustees of Amherst College from *The Poems of Emily Dickinson*, Thomas H. Johnson, ed., Cambridge, Mass.: The Belknap Press of Harvard University Press, Copyright ' 1951, 1955, 1979 by the President and Fellows of Harvard College.
16, 28. Carcanet Press Ltd for □On the Road to the Sea□ and □The Farmer□s Bride□ from *Collected Poems & Selected Prose* (1981) by Charlotte Mew.
24. □Black Woman□ is from *Pink Ladies in the Afternoon* by Naomi Long Madgett, published by Lotus Press, Inc, Detroit 1972. ' Naomi Long Madgett 1972.
30. Bloodaxe Books for □Julian of Norwich□ from *Mr & Mrs Scotland Are Dead: Poems 1980—1994* (Bloodaxe Books, 2002).
32. □Warming Her Pearls□ is taken from *Selling Manhattan* by Carol Ann Duffy, published by Anvil Poetry Press (1987).
33, 155. □First Fig□ and □Sonnet□ (□I, being born a woman and distressed□) by Edna St. Vincent Millay. From *Collected Poems*, HarperCollins. Copyright ' 1922, 1923, 1950, 1951 by Edna St. Vincent Millay and Norma Millay Ellis. All rights reserved. Reprinted by permission of Elizabeth Barnett, literary executor.
34. John Murray for □Myfanwy□ from *Collected Poems* by John Betjeman.
47. □She Walked Unaware□ is from *One Landscape Still* by Patrick MacDonogh, published by Secker & Warburg.
48. □Why She Says No□ is from *The Forces of Plenty* by Ellen Bryant Voigt, published by W.W. Norton & Company (1983).
49. Fragment Thirty-nine (□He is more than a hero□) is from *Sappho: A New Translation* by Mary Barnard, published by the University of California Press. Copyright ' 1958 The Regents of the University of California; ' renewed 1986 Mary Barnard. Reprinted by permission of the University of California Press.
52. □Maura□ is from *Grimalkin* by Thomas Lynch published by Jonathan Cape. Used by permission of The Random House Group Limited.
62. Carcanet Press Ltd for □Fragment Thirty-six□ from *Collected Poems* (1995) by H.D. (Hilda Doolittle).
65. Faber and Faber Ltd for □La Figlia che Piange□ from *Collected Poems 1909—1962* by T.S. Eliot.
72. David Higham Associates for □Sweat□ from *The Moon Disposes*, published by Secker & Warburg.
73. Faber and Faber Ltd for the extract from *The Dream Songs* by John Berryman.
78. Bloodaxe Books for □Desires□ from *Central Reservations* by Connie Bensley (Bloodaxe Books, 1990).
79. Faber and Faber Ltd for □Song□ from *If I Don□t Know* by Wendy Cope.
81. Faber and Faber Ltd for □Field Work□ from *Field Work* by Seamus Heaney.

84. □Those Women□ from *The Fat Black Woman□s Poems* by Grace Nichols is reproduced with permission of Curtis Brown Ltd, London, on behalf of Grace Nichols. Copyright ' Grace Nichols.
87, 89. Bloodaxe Books for □Privacy of Rain□ and □Dancing Man□ from *Out of the Blue: Poems 1975—2001* by Helen Dunmore (Bloodaxe Books, 2002).
88. Faber and Faber Ltd for □The Voice□ from *Collected Poems* by Theodore Roethke.
91. □The Fired Pot□ from *The Writings of Anna Wickham*, ed. R.D. Smith, is reprinted by permission of George W. Hepburn and Margaret Hepburn.
93. David Higham Associates for □Meeting Point□ from *Collected Poems* by Louis MacNeice, published by Faber and Faber Ltd.
95, 150. Carcanet Press Ltd for □Gift of Sight□ and □Symptoms of Love□ from *Collected Poems* (1975) by Robert Graves.
96. □The Shampoo□ is from *The Complete Poems 1927—1979* by Elizabeth Bishop. Copyright ' 1979, 1983 by Alice Helen Methfessel. Reprinted by permission of Farrar, Straus and Giroux, LLC.
97. Time Warner Books UK for □After□ from *The Complete Collected Poems of Maya Angelou* (Virago, 1994). Copyright ' 1994 Maya Angelou. Published by arrangement with Random House Inc.
98. □Possibly□ is from *Signs of Love* by Lesle□ Newman, published by Windstorm Creative, Ltd. Copyright ' 1991, 2000 by Lesle□ Newman. Reprinted by permission of Curtis Brown Ltd.
99. Faber and Faber Ltd for □September□ from *The Hawk in the Rain* by Ted Hughes.
110. Faber and Faber Ltd for □Siren Song□ from *Collected Poems* by Hugo Williams.
112. □Coat□ is from *Close Relatives* by Vicki Feaver, published by Secker & Warburg (1981).
113, 145. Carcanet Press Ltd for □One Cigarette□ and □Strawberries□ from *Collected Poems* (1982) by Edwin Morgan.
120. David Higham Associates for □One Flesh□ from *New Collected Poems* by Elizabeth Jennings, published by Carcanet Press Ltd.
125. The Estate of James MacGibbon for □Conviction□ by Stevie Smith.
127. □may I feel□ is reprinted from *Complete Poems 1904—1962* by E.E. Cummings, edited by George J. Firmage, by permission of W.W. Norton & Company. Copyright ' 1991 by the Trustees for the E.E. Cummings Trust and George James Firmage.
129. □The Jewels□ is translated by Roy Campbell from the original by Charles Baudelaire. Ad Donker Publishers, an imprint of Jonathan Ball Publishers, South Africa.
132. Carcanet Press Ltd for □Queen-Anne□s-Lace□ from *Collected Poems* (2000) by William Carlos Williams.
133. □The Fleece□ is from *Dark Ages* by David Hartnett published by Secker & Warburg. Used by permission of The Random House Group Limited.
134. □On a Night of the Full Moon□ is from *Chosen Poems: Old and New* by Audre Lord. Copyright ' 1982, 1976, 1974, 1973, 1970, 1968 by Audre Lord. Used by permission of W.W. Norton & Company (1982).
136. Faber and Faber Ltd for □Lovesong□ from *Crow* by Ted Hughes.
138. □The Time Before You□ is from *On Ballycastle Beach* by Mebdh McGuckian. Reprinted by kind permission of the author and The Gallery Press, Loughcrew, Oldcastle, County Meath, Ireland.
141. □Intimacy□ is from *Collected Poems* by Edgell Rickword published by Bodley Head. Used by permission of The Random House Group Limited.

142. 'Making Love' is from *Wellspring* by Sharon Olds published by Jonathan Cape. Used by permission of The Random House Group Limited.
144. Faber and Faber Ltd for 'The Muse' from *Her Book* by Jo Shapcott.
152. A.P. Watt Ltd on behalf of Michael B. Yeats for 'Leda and the Swan' from *The Collected Poems of W.B. Yeats*.
156. Pollinger Limited and the Estate of Frieda Lawrence Ravagli for 'Desire' from *The Complete Poems of D.H. Lawrence*.
167. 'Sabbath Bells' by John Clare is reproduced with permission of Curtis Brown Group, London on behalf of Eric Robinson. © Eric Robinson 1996.
170. Carcanet Press Ltd for 'Still-life' from *Collected Poems* (1976) by Elizabeth Daryush.
171. Bloodaxe Books for 'Moules à la Marinière' from *The Rule of Three* by Elizabeth Garrett (Bloodaxe Books, 1991).
172. 'The Centaur' by May Swenson is used with permission of The Literary Estate of May Swenson.
175. 'The Sisters' from *The Collected Poems of Roy Campbell* is reprinted with the permission of Ad Donker Publishers, an imprint of Jonathan Ball Ball Publishers, South Africa.

INDEX OF POETS' NAMES

— ◇ —

INDEX OF FIRST LINES

— ◇ —